Computers, Information, Awareness
a practical course

Peter Ayre
and
Tony Payne

STUDENTS BOOK

Pitman

PITMAN PUBLISHING LIMITED
128 Long Acre, London WC2E 9AN

Associated Companies
Pitman Publishing New Zealand Ltd,
Wellington
Pitman Publishing Pty Ltd, Melbourne

ISBN 0 273 01996 1

Printed in Great Britain
at The Pitman Press, Bath

Contents

To the student

This book examines six examples of the use of computers in everyday situations. Each shows the way in which computers process data and produce information.

In every case the computer application is accompanied by a program which, when run on your microcomputer, illustrates some of the important features. The computing concepts and the hardware involved are described and explained, and you will be asked to think about some of the issues raised and answer some questions about them.

Your teacher will make the software available for you and provide you with sufficient instructions to enable you to use it. It is important that you gain some experience of operating the computer, as well as observing what happens when other students take their turn. As a result of using this text you should become more aware of the effect of computers on the world around you, effects that are likely to increase, whether as part of your work or of your leisure.

SHOP

Increasingly, computers are being used by shops in order to become more efficient and to improve customer service. Computers can be used to keep records of sales, sales trends and stock levels. They can also be used for accounting. The information produced by the computer helps managers with decision-making.

TYPE OF BOOK	TITLE
ENGLISH LANGUAGE	ESSENTIAL SPELLING LIST
COOKERY	GOURMET COOKING FOR VEGETARIANS
GENERAL FICTION	1984
SCIENCE FICTION	PERILOUS PLANETS
SCIENCE FICTION	CASTLE ROOGNA
SCIENCE FICTION	GODS OF MARS
GENERAL FICTION	1984
COOKERY	CORDON BLEU COOKERY
GENERAL FICTION	GIRL IN A SWING
GENERAL FICTION	LEVKAS MAN
GENERAL FICTION	NORTH STAR
MUSIC	WHATEVER HAPPENED TO
GENERAL FICTION	1984
CINEMA	HISTORY OF THE SILENT SCREEN
SCIENCE FICTION	PRINCESS OF MARS
SCIENCE FICTION	WARLORDS OF MARS
COOKERY	COOKING IN A BEDSITTER
GENERAL FICTION	THE SHINING
GENERAL FICTION	1984
SCIENCE FICTION	GENESIS MACHINE
THEATRE	FIVE PLAYS
GENERAL FICTION	1984
GENERAL FICTION	THE TRIAL
SCIENCE FICTION	SECOND TRIP
CINEMA	CLINT EASTWOOD
COMPUTING	MICROFUTURE
COOKERY	CLASSIC ITALIAN COOKBOOK
GENERAL FICTION	1984
DICTIONARY	COLLINS SPANISH DICTIONARY
MATHEMATICS	FOUR FIGURE MATHS TABLE
COMPUTING	INTRODUCTION TO BASIC
MILITARY	HISTORY OF THE US AIRFORCE
GENERAL FICTION	SOUND AND THE FURY
PHOTOGRAPHY	COLOUR PHOTOGRAPHY
GENERAL FICTION	THE SHINING
COMPUTING	INTRODUCTION TO BASIC

Fig 1.1 Record of daily sales

AUTHOR	PRICE	METHOD OF PAYMENT
SCHONELL F	0.95	CASH
CLARK R	1.35	CASH
ORWELL G	1.25	CASH
ALDISS B	1.95	CREDIT CARD
ANTHONY P	1.50	CASH
BURROUGHS G	1.50	CASH
ORWELL G	1.25	CASH
HUME R	2.50	CREDIT CARD
ADAMS R	2.25	CREDIT CARD
INNES H	1.95	CASH
INNES H	1.75	CASH
ELSON H	7.95	CHEQUE
ORWELL G	1.25	CASH
BLUM D	6.95	CHEQUE
BURROUGHS G	1.50	CASH
BURROUGHS G	1.50	CASH
WHITEHORN K	1.95	CASH
KING S	2.25	CREDIT CARD
ORWELL G	1.25	CASH
HOGAN J	1.95	CASH
CHEKOV A	1.95	CASH
ORWELL G	1.25	CASH
KAFKA F	1.75	CASH
SILVERBERG	1.95	CREDIT CARD
DOWNING	4.45	CHEQUE
SHELLEY J	3.50	CHEQUE
HAZAN M	4.50	CASH
ORWELL G	1.25	CASH
	8.95	CASH
CASTLE F	1.35	CASH
HARTLEY P	3.45	CHEQUE
ANDERTON D	9.95	CREDIT CARD
FAULKNER W	2.45	CASH
NUTTING L	4.95	CASH
KING S	2.25	CASH
HARTLEY P	3.45	CASH

This chapter examines how a computer can be used for stock control in a bookshop and a chain store. Before doing so however, it will be useful to look at how **data** can be **processed** to produce **information**.

Squeezing the data

The titles of books sold in a single day in a bookshop are listed in Fig. 1.1. They were recorded, along with other details about the book and method of payment, as each sale was made. We can look upon these details as raw data. Below are some tasks designed to produce information from the data.

You might try completing these tasks within a time limit and comparing your answers with those of the rest of the class. Suggested times:
1) 15 sec, 2) 2 min, 3) 4 min, 4) 20 sec, 5) 2 min.

1	How many books were sold during the day?
2	How much was paid by credit card?
3	How much was paid in cash?
4	How many types of book were sold?
5	How many of each type were sold?
6	How many copies of *1984* were sold. How many copies of *The Shining* were sold? How many copies of *Introduction to Basic* were sold?

Did everyone get an answer for every task? Were your answers always accurate? Could the tasks be described as difficult? What other information could you squeeze from this data?

You might think that knowing how many copies of individual titles were sold is not very useful. In fact, it is the key to a complex system. This is an example of information which can be used as data in another process. It can be used to generate a chain of information upon which decisions can be based.

The first step in this process is to work out how many copies of each title sold are actually left in stock at the end of the day. Fig. 1.2 is a list of the titles used in the exercise "squeezing the data". Beside each one is a record of the stock status at the beginning of the day (0900 hrs). Work out the stock status at the close of trading (1800 hrs). Instead of writing down the titles, use the code numbers to identify the books (1 for *History of the Silent Screen*, 2 for *Clint Eastwood*, etc.). Produce a table like the one in Fig. 1.3.

CODE	TITLE	STOCK 0900 hrs
1.	HISTORY OF THE SILENT SCREEN	1
2.	CLINT EASTWOOD	1
3.	GOURMET COOKING FOR VEGETARIANS	3
4.	CLASSIC ITALIAN COOKBOOK	2
5.	CORDON BLEU COOKERY	1
6.	COOKING IN A BEDSITTER	2
7.	INTRODUCTION TO BASIC	4
8.	MICROFUTURE	4
9.	COLLINS SPANISH DICTIONARY	3
10.	ESSENTIAL SPELLING LIST	3
11.	GIRL IN A SWING	5
12.	SOUND AND THE FURY	2
13.	LEVKAS MAN	3
14.	NORTH STAR	4
15.	THE SHINING	3
16.	THE TRIAL	3
17.	1984	9
18.	FOUR FIGURE MATHS TABLES	3
19.	HISTORY OF THE US AIRFORCE	1
20.	WHATEVER HAPPENED TO	2
21.	COLOUR PHOTOGRAPHY	2
22.	PERILOUS PLANETS	5
23.	CASTLE ROOGNA	4
24.	GODS OF MARS	6
25.	PRINCESS OF MARS	4
26.	WARLORDS OF MARS	5
27.	GENESIS MACHINE	7
28.	SECOND TRIP	6
29.	FIVE PLAYS	3

Fig 1.2   Record of opening stock

CODE	STOCK 0900 hrs	NUMBER SOLD	STOCK 1800 hrs
1	1	1	0
2	1	1	0
3	3	1	2
4	2	?	?
29	3	?	?

Fig 1.3

Data processing

So far, the processing of data which you have done has been reasonably simple. You have had to count, do simple addition and subtraction. Most people would not regard these tasks as difficult but they are time-consuming, and under pressure mistakes are often made.

Imagine having to go through this process in order to maintain an up-to-date record of stock levels. It would be far too time-consuming to be practical. A possible alternative might be to use a card index. A 3 inch by 5 inch card could be used for each title (Fig. 1.4) and the cards could be arranged in some sort of order, perhaps alphabetically by title. Each time a purchase is made, the book's card could be found. The stock level printed on the card could be changed (updated) by the sales assistant and the card returned to its place in the filing cabinet.

Although possible, this still is not very satisfactory. It would require a large number of cards to cover the stock of a bookshop with around 10 000 titles. What is more, having kept a perfect record of stock levels, all of this information would be completely locked in a card index. It would be very time-consuming to check, for example, which titles are out of stock.

An answer might be to use a computer. A suitable computer with an appropriate program can be used to store and update instantly the electronic equivalent of the 3 by 5 inch cards. In addition, the computer can very easily squeeze the data in the records to produce information.

In the next section we run a program called Top Ten. It simulates, in a small way, stock control in a record shop.

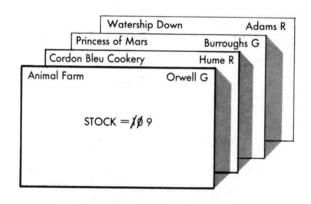

Fig 1.4 Card-index record

Top Ten

THE BEATLES
stereo
PARLOPHONE
ELVIS COSTELLO
Neil Young
IN FLIGHT
GEORGE BENSON
THE POLICE
Outlandos d'Amour
BOB
DYLAN
BLOOD
ON
THE
TRACKS
THE
DARK SIDE
OF THE
MOON
David Bowie
GRACE JONES / NIGHTCLUBBING
CULTURE CLUB
COLOUR BY NUMBERS

Top Ten is a program designed to show the computer coping with some of the processing problems which you have experienced so far. The purpose is to establish a *file* of album titles, which represent a shop's stock, and then to make purchases from that stock. The com- puter will keep an up-to-date record of sales, stock and income and this information will be presented in a screen display (Fig. 1.5). The data collected can then be squeezed to produce more information.

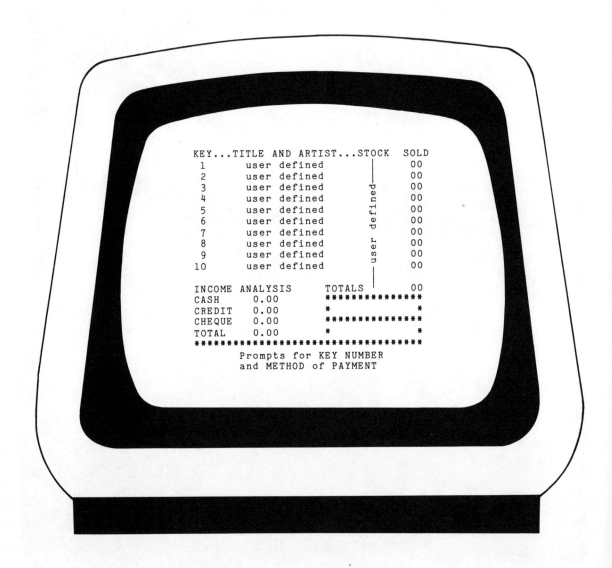

```
KEY...TITLE AND ARTIST...STOCK   SOLD
  1      user defined              00
  2      user defined              00
  3      user defined              00
  4      user defined              00
  5      user defined              00
  6      user defined              00
  7      user defined              00
  8      user defined              00
  9      user defined              00
 10      user defined              00

INCOME ANALYSIS      TOTALS        00
CASH      0.00      ***************
CREDIT    0.00      *             *
CHEQUE    0.00      ***************
TOTAL     0.00      *             *
***************************************
        Prompts for KEY NUMBER
        and METHOD of PAYMENT
```

Fig 1.5 Screen display for album titles, sales and stock

File creation

The first part of the whole program is concerned with file creation and has three parts:

1 All records in the shop have the same price, in the range £1.00 to £9.99. Decide upon a sensible standard price and input this, in response to the prompt, in pennies. Then press RETURN for further data entry.

2 Ten titles (and artists) must be input to complete the file. The prompt is

```
TITLE AND ARTIST
<...................>
```

25 characters are allowed for title and artist. It may be necessary to use abbreviations. (Press RETURN for data entry.)
   Input a stock level for each title in response to the prompt:

```
STOCK LEVEL
Input a whole number in range 10-15
```

An opportunity is provided to correct the record entry. The message:

```
RECORD OK? INPUT Y or N
```

will appear. Y means yes; N means no. If you input the character Y, the record will be accepted. If you input the character N, the whole record can be input again.

3 When all 10 titles have been input, the computer will invite you to indicate a stock level at which a reorder message is required. This is in the range 1–9.
   During the program run, the computer will flash the message

```
REORDER
```

on the screen when the stock of any LP falls to this level.

Sales

As soon as the reorder level has been input, the program moves to the transaction stage. Records can be purchased and the method of payment indicated. The two prompts are:

```
Input key
A whole number in range 1-10
```

(Press RETURN for data entry.)

```
Method of payment
1) Cash, 2) Credit, 3) Cheque
Input 1, 2 or 3
```

(Press RETURN for data entry.)

   After each input, the screen display will change to show current stock status, sales and income totals.

Procedure
a   One member of the class should take on the role of shopkeeper and input the data.
b   Each member of the class should purchase a record (two if time permits).
c   While transactions are taking place, observe the changes in the screen display.

Reports

When each person has purchased as many records as time permits, STOP can be input instead of a key number. This tells the computer that trading has ceased for the day.
   A menu of Report Options will appear. The data which has been collected during the sales' period can now be squeezed to produce information. Decide which reports will provide the following information:

• The Top Ten.
• Those records which have sold no copies today. [There are 2 ways of doing this.]
• A list of records which have sold at least 1 copy today.
• A complete inventory in alphabetical order.
• A list of records which are out of stock.
• A list of records for which stock has dropped below the reorder level defined during file creation.

```
THE SHINING          KING S              NEW ENGLISH LIBRARY
ISBN 0450049744      PAPERBACK           PRICE=2.25
SOLD THIS YEAR=93    SOLD THIS MONTH=8     SOLD TODAY=2
SOLD
  OCT . NOV . DEC . JAN . FEB . MAR . APR . MAY . JUN . JUL . AUG
   6    10     6     7     6     8    11     8     7     9     7

STOCK IN HAND=5      QUANTITY ON ORDER=6
```

Fig 1.6   Information held in a typical computer record

Updating Computer records

Just as the computer can maintain a record of stock and sales for albums, so it can for books. It can hold, on a magnetic disk, one computer record for each book in stock (see Fig. 1.6). A **computer record** is all of the data about one item. A collection of computer records is called a **file**.

As a book is sold, the computer locates the appropriate record and takes 1 away from the stock-in-hand total. It also adds 1 to each of the following totals: sold this year, sold this month, sold today. In this way it keeps an up-to-date record of sales and stock for each title. This is called **updating** a computer record. The computer can also store the sales totals for each of the previous 11 months (more if you wish). The manager can then see the "sales trend" for the previous year and can use all of this information as a basis for taking decisions about the reordering of stock.

People need notes on a computer record, like "sold this year" and "sold this month", so that they know what the figures mean. The compu-ter, however, knows what the data is from the *position* of the data in the record. The compu-ter's view of the record is as shown in Fig. 1.7.

Each item of data in the example is sepa-rated by a comma. Although the monthly sales totals in Fig. 1.6 are headed OCT, NOV, DEC, etc., the computer regards them as sales 11 months ago, 10 months ago, and 9 months ago, etc. At the end of each month, the figure in position 10 is replaced by the figure in position 11, which is replaced by the figure in position 12, and so on. The data in the 20th position is replaced by the sold-this-month figure (8 in our example) and then the sold-this-month figure is set to zero to start the new month afresh.

If we imagine that Fig. 1.7 is the record for the last day in September, the record will look like Fig. 1.8 when updated for October trad-ing.

The letters ISBN (see next section) do not appear in the record and the Letter P is the 5th item of data. Why?

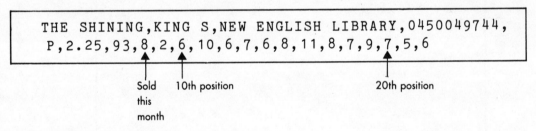

Fig 1.7 Computer's view of book record

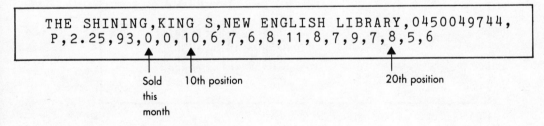

Fig 1.8 Updated book record in the computer

International standard book number (ISBN) As a book is sold, the stock-in-hand and sold-today totals must be updated immediately so that any inquiries will be answered with accurate information. The computer must find the correct record and make the necessary adjustments. It might be tempting to locate a record by book title or author's name, with the computer looking for a record containing the title or name input. This approach can give rise to problems. Many non-fiction books have the same title, and some authors have the same surname and initial. A better method is to use a book's International Standard Book Number (ISBN). Every published title has its own unique ISBN

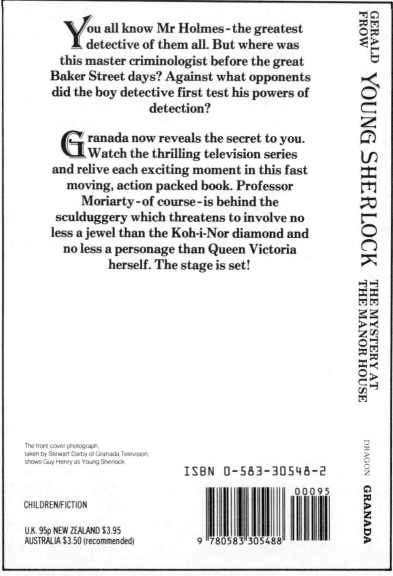

You all know Mr Holmes - the greatest detective of them all. But where was this master criminologist before the great Baker Street days? Against what opponents did the boy detective first test his powers of detection?

Granada now reveals the secret to you. Watch the thrilling television series and relive each exciting moment in this fast moving, action packed book. Professor Moriarty - of course - is behind the sculduggery which threatens to involve no less a jewel than the Koh-i-Nor diamond and no less a personage than Queen Victoria herself. The stage is set!

GERALD FROW
YOUNG SHERLOCK
THE MYSTERY AT THE MANOR HOUSE
DRAGON GRANADA

The front cover photograph, taken by Stewart Darby of Granada Television, shows Guy Henry as Young Sherlock.

CHILDREN/FICTION

U.K. 95p NEW ZEALAND $3.95
AUSTRALIA $3.50 (recommended)

ISBN 0-583-30548-2

00095

9 780583 305488

Fig 1.9 Book cover showing the ISBN (and the full information required for sales-recording in bar code form)

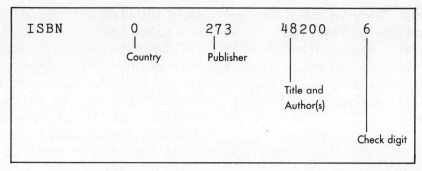

Fig 1.10 International standard book number

allocated to it, so that no two different publications should have the same number.

The ISBN appears on the inside of the book and also, for the convenience of sales staff, on the back cover (Fig. 1.9).

When a book is sold, the assistant can key the ISBN into the computer or use a wand (Fig. 1.13) to read the number automatically. The computer is programmed to "jump" to the correct record instantly, even though there may be thousands of records.

The ISBN is a 10-figure code, made up of 4 groups of numbers. The first is a country code. For example, the code for the UK, USA, Irish Republic, New Zealand, Australia and Canada is 0 (zero). France uses the identifier 2, Germany 3, and the Netherlands 90. The next number is the publisher's code, unique to each publisher. The third number is for the particular book title and author. The final number is a single digit known as a "check digit" (Fig. 1.10). It is used to check the accuracy of the number, when used in a computer system.

Calculation of a check digit

When the first 9 digits are allocated, a calculation is performed on them to determine the value of the check digit.

1   Each digit is multiplied by its *weight*. The weights are values from 10 to 2, as follows:

ISBN	0	2	7	3	4	8	2	0	0
×	×	×	×	×	×	×	×	×	×
	10	9	8	7	6	5	4	3	2
	0	18	56	21	24	40	8	0	0

2   The results are added:

$$0 + 18 + 56 + 21 + 24 + 40 + 8 + 0 + 0 = 167$$

3   The result is divided by 11:
$$\frac{167}{11} = 15 \text{ remainder } 2$$

4   The remainder is subtracted from 11. The result is the check digit.
$$11 - 2 = 9$$

The check digit is 9.

Sometimes a result of 10 is obtained for the check digit. If so, then since an ISBN must always contain ten characters only, the check digit is recorded with the capital letter X.

So the complete ISBN is
0 273 48200 9

Data validation When the ISBN is entered into the computer, either by keying in or by an OCR wand, the computer performs a similar calculation to the one described. If the check digit cannot be generated from the other nine digits, the ISBN is rejected and an error message is output.

---

1 What will the check digits be for each of the following:
  ISBN 0 273 01583?
  ISBN 0 273 01272?

2 Will the computer accept this ISBN:
  0 273 01676 4?

3 What do you think the check digit will be if the remainder after division by 11 is zero?

4 In what other system might a check digit be useful?

Information

The principal aim of a business is "to make a profit". In fact, we might go further and say "to maximise profit". In order to do this, a bookshop must maximise its sales by having the books that the customer wants, when they are wanted. It must not miss opportunities to sell. Shelves must be well stocked, but not overstocked with the wrong books. When dealing with thousands (sometimes tens of thousands) of different titles, this is not easy to accomplish.

Consider this example. Ten copies of a book are received by the bookshop on 1 April. They cost the bookseller £2.00 each. They will be sold for £3.00 each. By 30 April all of the books are sold. The shop has made a profit of £10.00. A stock check on 31 May reveals that the book is out of stock (Fig. 1.11).

The key question is: how many more could have been sold between 30 April and the time that the reordered stock arrives sometime after 31 May? If the out-of-stock situation had been revealed earlier, the original £20.00 could then, perhaps, have been re-invested in ten more copies of the same title. If all of those had been sold by 31 May, the original £20.00 would have earned £20.00 instead of £10.00 in the same period.

In order to restock with the right number of the right titles at the right time, it is necessary to have up-to-date information frequently. It is difficult and very time-consuming to obtain this by manual checking. The computer, however, can provide it, if it is continuously fed with the data from all transactions throughout the day.

At the end of each day, a report can be printed listing the stock, orders and sales trend for each title sold during the day. The manager can use this information to decide – on a daily basis – whether or not to "top up" the stock of a particular title.

1 APRIL	INVESTMENT	RETAIL PRICE	30 APRIL	INCOME	PROFIT	31 MAY
New Stock 10 books @2.00	£20.00	£3.00 each	Out of Stock	£30.00	£10.00	Stock Check reveals out-of-stock

Fig 1.11 Stock check

14

Book Sales Report

3 Sept

```
MY SON MY SON              SPRING H                FONTANA
ISBN 0006123066            PAPERBACK               PRICE=1.25
SOLD THIS YEAR=1           SOLD THIS MONTH=1       SOLD TODAY=1
SOLD:
  OCT . NOV . DEC. JAN . FEB . MAR . APR . MAY . JUN . JUL . AUG
   0     0     0    0      0     0     0     0     0     0     0
STOCK IN HAND=0            QUANTITY ON ORDER=0


1984                       ORWELL G                PENGUIN
ISBN 0140017003            PAPERBACK               PRICE=1.25
SOLD THIS YEAR=57          SOLD THIS MONTH=8       SOLD TODAY=6
SOLD:
  OCT . NOV . DEC. JAN . FEB . MAR . APR . MAY . JUN . JUL . AUG
   0     0     5    2      4     8    11     3     1     9     6
STOCK IN HAND=3            QUANTITY ON ORDER=0


TITUS GROAN                PEAKE M                 PENGUIN
ISBN 0140027629            PAPERBACK               PRICE=1.75
SOLD THIS YEAR=17          SOLD THIS MONTH=1       SOLD TODAY=1
SOLD:
  OCT . NOV . DEC. JAN . FEB . MAR . APR . MAY . JUN . JUL . AUG
   2     0     1    2      3     2     3     2     0     1     1
STOCK IN HAND=0            QUANTITY ON ORDER=0


WOMAN WARRIOR              KINGSTON M              PAN
ISBN 0330264001            PAPERBACK               PRICE=1.50
SOLD THIS YEAR=11          SOLD THIS MONTH=1       SOLD TODAY=1
SOLD:
  OCT . NOV . DEC. JAN . FEB . MAR . APR . MAY . JUN . JUL . AUG
   1     1     2    1      0     1     1     2     0     1     0
STOCK IN HAND=1            QUANTITY ON ORDER=2
```

Fig 1.12 Book sales analysis

If you were the manager, which of the four titles shown in the part sales report in Fig. 1.12 would you:

a delete from stock?
b order none for the time being?
c order 2 copies?
d order 6 copies?

When making your decisions look at the sales trend, stock in hand, and quantity on order, in each record. Be prepared to give reasons for your decisions.

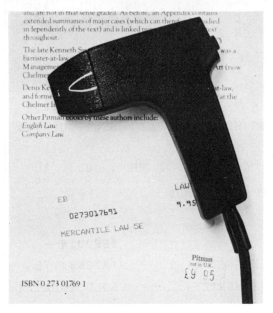

Fig 1.13 OCR-A reader, used at point-of-sale terminal

Point-of-sale data capture

An **optical character recognition reader** scans each character on the surface of a document with a beam of light. The reader examines the light reflected back to it from the surface, and by doing this it identifies the shape of each character it has scanned. Each shape is then compared with a set of stored patterns. If a positive character identification is made, the data is accepted.

The type of wand used to read ISBNs and other product codings is illustrated in Fig. 1.13. One commonly used type is described as an OCR A-wand. The A indicates that it reads a specific typeface – the American National Standard (Fig. 1.14).

The complete computer system

Fig. 1.15 shows a typical system as used in bookshops, and shops generally. The description that follows is based on a typical bookshop operation, as shown in the illustration.

Fig 1.14 Optical type-font OCR-A

```
ABCDEFGHIJKLMNOPQRS
TUVWXYZ0123456789.,
'-{}%?ſ¥Н:;=+/$*"&
```

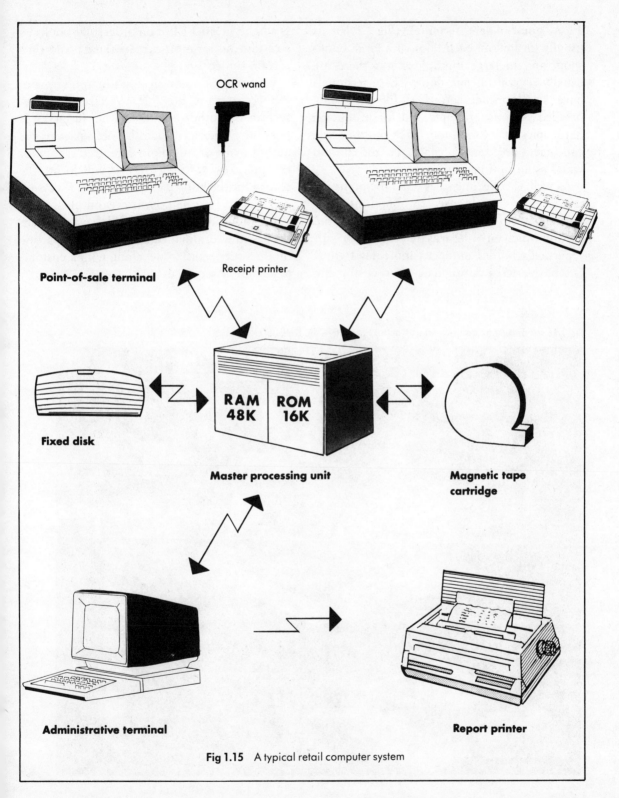

OCR wand

Receipt printer

Point-of-sale terminal

Fixed disk

RAM 48K **ROM 16K**

Master processing unit

Magnetic tape cartridge

Administrative terminal

Report printer

Fig 1.15 A typical retail computer system

1 A **point-of-sale terminal** (Fig. 1.16) is usually located on each floor of a large bookshop, and in large multiple stores there are usually several on one floor. These terminals have small printers attached for producing detailed customer receipts and for producing hardcopies of information. Each point-of-sale can have an optical character recognition wand as an optional input device.

As well as collecting sales data, the point-of-sale terminals can be used to obtain information about stock status, books on order, the date on which an order was placed, books with a particular order number, and sales trends. Often, queries will originate from customers.

Is a book in stock? Is it on order? Are books by a certain author in stock? Are there books on a certain subject?

Customers do not usually think in terms of ISBNs, so it is possible to retrieve master records by author or title as well. In fact, it is possible to retrieve them by only part of the author name or title. For example, a search for the title *The Nationwide Pro* will locate the record for the book *The Nationwide Provision and Use of Information*, if it is on file.

In addition to dealing with customer inquiries, the terminal can be used to put a title on the order/reorder file, along with a customer's name if required.

Fig 1.16   A bookshop point-of-sale terminal (as used in the DUET system)

2 An **administrative terminal** is situated in the stockroom. It controls the system and is used to process incoming stock. The computer holds details of orders, and balances these against stock received. As the arrival of a book is logged, a label is automatically produced by a dot matrix printer (see p. 96) linked to the terminal. This label has printed on it machine-readable characters (since not all books carry these at present) and included are: title, author, ISBN, price, and shelf-location code. If the book has been ordered specially for a particular customer, the customer's name will also be printed on the label so that the order is identified, and so that the customer can be informed. The printer is also used for producing a range of reports.

3 Data is stored in a **disk store** on a Winchester fixed sealed disk (see p. 66) with a capacity of 12.5 megabytes. It can hold records for 25 000 stock items. The system can be expanded to a 4-disk system with 100 megabytes of backing store.

A megabyte is 2^{20} bytes, i.e. 1 048 576 bytes.

A kilobyte is 2^{10} bytes, i.e. 1024 bytes. One kilobyte is usually abbreviated to 1 K.

4 Magnetic tape back-up A magnetic tape cartridge (see p. 61) is used as back-up for the fixed disc. The master records are "dumped" (copied) at convenient intervals so that the shop is in a position to recover from a system breakdown. In practice, dumping usually takes place once a week only – because it is a slow process. An alternative, but much more expensive, method of back-up is to use duplicate disks. Dumping from disk to disk is a much faster operation.

Information

A **master record** exists for each title. It is 242 characters long and contains 50 pieces of data, including:

- Title
- Author
- Publisher
- Prices: publisher's list price; actual selling price
- VAT rating (if any)
- Purchase ordering information: quantity on order; quantity on order cancelled; purchase order number; method of shipment desired; date to cancel or chase order; identification of customer special order
- Stock figure
- Sales figures: today; this week; this month; this year; each of the last 13 months
- Purchase order history: invoice number; last supplier; discount on invoice; date received; date of invoice
- Customer special order: name; telephone number.

This data can be retrieved as it stands, or squeezed to produce information. Among the reports which might be generated are:

- A daily sales analysis (similar to Fig. 1.12)
- Orders outstanding: by a particular supplier; by the date placed; before a given date
- VAT summaries
- Inventory lists: full (perhaps for annual stocktaking); partial (organised by type of book or publisher, for example)
- Lists of best-sellers: books with sales figures above a certain level
- Lists of slow movers: books with sales figures below a given level.

mothercare

Kimball tags

If you visit a Mothercare shop, you will see that some goods have a card tag attached to them (Fig. 1.17a). The name given to these is Kimball Tag. They carry four pieces of information: a product code, a colour code, a size code, and the price. This information is printed for the benefit of the sales assistant and customer but is coded in binary (zeros and ones) for the benefit of a computer. The binary code appears as a series of punched holes.

When an item is sold, the sales assistant removes the tag and puts it on a spike (Fig. 1.18). At the end of the week, the tags are secured on the spike and sent off to Mothercare's computer centre, where the information on them is read into a computer. The spike carries a branch code so that the computer centre knows to which store the tags belong.

The computer uses this information to prepare a replacement order for each item sold. As well as printing an order for the supplier, it prints new tags for each item ordered. The shop's stock record is updated at the same time. The computer also prints a report for the shop, listing the goods which will shortly be received. In this way, the staff will not be taken by surprise and customers can be kept informed of delivery dates.

The process is illustrated in Fig. 1.19.

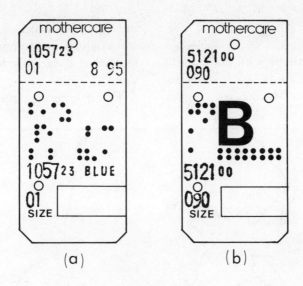

Fig 1.17 Kimball Tag as used by Mothercare

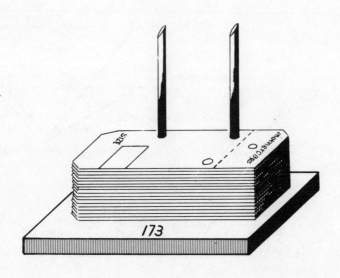

Fig 1.18 Mothercare spike

Accuracy of records

The emphasis in bookshops is on maintaining up-to-date accurate records as a basis for reordering. With the Mothercare system, however, the records are rarely accurate. The stock which the computer thinks a shop has and what it actually has are not always the same.

This may result simply from the fact that an

Fig 1.19 A computer-based system for stock and tag replacement

assistant has failed to spike a tag. It is more likely to result from the fact that customers exchange goods. For example, father is sent to the shop to buy a particular item. He gets the right item, the correct colour . . . but the wrong size. When the item was sold, the tag was spiked. The computer subsequently recorded a sale. When the item is exchanged for the correct size, this new tag is spiked too. The returned item is given a handwritten tag and displayed for sale. No attempt is made to delete the previous sale from the computer's records.

The emphasis here is on a fast turn-round of orders, not on absolute accuracy. The computer records are adjusted four times a year when the shop carries out a complete stock-check. Even then, because the shop carries thousands of different products, only the large differences are adjusted – based on numbers or price. A discrepancy of 100 bars of soap is unlikely to be adjusted; a discrepancy of two £80.00 prams will be.

Bulk tags

If the Kimball Tag is the key to fast reordering, why don't all Mothercare items carry them? Much of Mothercare stock is standard: they will always sell nappies, soap, talcum powder, and so on. Because of this, the store receives bulk packages of these items. The package carries a single tag marked with the letter B in blue (Fig. 1.17b). When the package is opened and the goods put on display, this tag is spiked. By the end of the week the computer will have recorded sales for each item in the package, even though most of them may still be on the shelf. Obviously, as they are sold, what the computer thinks the shop has sold and what it actually has sold will come closer and closer.

Information

The computer readily produces reports to assist the manager with decision-making. One of these reports will concern trends. If, say, yellow towels are selling better than any other colour, the computer will inform the manager in the report. Shortly after receiving this report, more shelf space will be given to yellow towels. If the colour trend changes, the display will change accordingly.

During the summer, more disposable nappies are bought. Mothers are on holiday, they don't want the chore of washing nappies, and certainly don't want to carry soiled ones around in hot weather. Some time in September the trend changes. Mothers go back to using washable nappies, or Terrys as they are called. An astute manager will be aware of this and can be expected to react to the situation. However, it might take a week or two to detect the change. During that time, opportunities to sell Terrys could have been lost. The computer identifies the change immediately. As a result, subtle changes will be made in the store. More space will gradually be given to Terrys than to disposable nappies. The position of the two types relative to the entrance to the shop is also likely to change; customers will reach the Terrys first. Given the correct information, the manager can make many such changes.

At about the same time as mothers change their preference for nappies, the computer will be fooled about another trend. Autumn lines will have arrived. Anxious to make them available to customers, perhaps before other stores do so, the manager ensures that they are on display in the shop. Many of these may be in bulk packages – the item is standard but is in "this year's colour". Because the tags are spiked before any sale is made, the computer will report that sky-blue-pink so and so's are selling very well at the moment! Here the human factor is important. The manager must intelligently interpret the information which the computer provides. For the time being, sky-blue-pink so and so's will not be given greater prominence.

Part of a weekly report produced by the computer is shown in Fig. 1.20. It lists items under two headings: Footwear, and Socks and Tights. These are in order of sale. Red wellingtons, for example, have sold better than other footwear. Black plimsolls take second place in this category, while blue trainers have sold fewer than any other type of footwear.

The manager of the shop can use this information to decide how much Sales Width (display space) to give each item. Red wellingtons have been allocated 2 units of display space. Blue trainers, however, are allocated only $\frac{3}{4}$ of a unit.

```
|===================================================|
| DEPARTMENT          £ PER   £000    SALES    WIDTHS|
|                                    ----------------|
| 8 FOOTWEAR SOCKS T  £68.42          £753        40 |
| ------------------------   ------   ---------------|
|    AVGE £PER WIDTH    £ 19                          |
|                            ------                  |
```

8.1 FOOTWEAR			£	IDEAL	ACT.
4447 WELLINGTON	RED	£3.68	40	2	
4453 PLIMSOLL BL	BLCK	£3.54	39	2	
4448 WELLINGTON	NAVY	£3.00	33	$1\frac{3}{4}$	
4475 SLIPPER MOON		£2.83	31	$1\frac{1}{2}$	
4446 SLIPPER BOOTEE C		£2.79	31	$1\frac{1}{2}$	
4440 WELLINGTON	RED	£2.17	24	$1\frac{1}{4}$	
4455 SHOE GINGHAM T B		£1.90	21	1	
4471 SLIPPERS BR	RED	£1.68	18	1	
4447 TRAINER NYL	BLUE	£1.53	17	$\frac{3}{4}$	
SUB GROUP TOTAL		£28.71	316	16	

8.2 SOCKS AND TIGHTS			£	IDEAL	ACT.
4239 SOCK MERCER	WHTE	£3.83	42	$2\frac{1}{4}$	
4392 TIGHTS NYLO	WHTE	£3.05	34	$1\frac{3}{4}$	
4259 SOCKS WOOL	GREY	£2.15	24	$1\frac{1}{4}$	
4704 SOCKS PATTE	GREY	£2.13	23	$1\frac{1}{4}$	
4261 SOCKS CROCH	WHTE	£1.95	21	1	
4260 SOCKS ACRYL	NAVY	£1.77	19	1	
4336 TIGHTS CABL	WHTE	£1.76	19	1	
4332 TIGHTS CABL	TUSK	£1.73	19	1	
4354 TIGHTS CABL	DAMS	£1.67	18	1	
SUB GROUP TOTAL		£34.55	380	20	

Fig 1.20 Weekly sales report

Fig. 1.21 shows a sales assistant using a wand to read bar codes. We can use this as the starting place for a short project.

1 Write a paragraph or two to answer each of the following questions:
  a Exactly what is the assistant doing? Describe her job.
  b What data is being collected? How often is it collected?
  c What happens to the data once it is collected?
  d Who uses the data, and how?

2 Are check digits a feature of this system? At what points in the process are they used?
3 Describe and illustrate the hardware used.
4 Illustrate your written work with as many photographs, drawings and diagrams as you can.

It may not be possible to describe any single system. The one that you write about should be representative. You can collect information by reading textbooks and manufacturers' brochures, and by interviewing staff in shops – make sure that you ask the manager first!

Fig 1.21

2 ONLINE INFORMATION

Your teacher should have brought to the lesson a set of documents about pollution. The word "document" is used to describe a source of information. This might be a book extract, booklet, pamphlet, newspaper article, magazine article, journal article, report, fact sheet, audio cassette, video cassette, set of slides, filmstrip, etc.

Assume that you have been given the task of writing an essay on water pollution, and in particular on the effects of industrial waste. One person in the class should attempt to select useful documents for the essay from the document collection provided by your teacher. We don't want the lesson to last all day, so

we'll set a time limit – 60 seconds. See how many useful documents one person can select in the time. Make a note of the number found.

You might share out the documents amongst the class and check to see if those selected were, in fact, about industrial waste as a water pollutant and whether any useful documents were overlooked.

Access to documents can be improved by indexing them. This involves preparing a collection of references, one for each document. The format of references varies from system to system, but a useful one can be seen in Fig. 2.1. The reference has five parts:

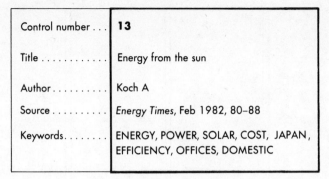

Control number . . .	**13**
Title	Energy from the sun
Author	Koch A
Source	*Energy Times*, Feb 1982, 80–88
Keywords	ENERGY, POWER, SOLAR, COST, JAPAN, EFFICIENCY, OFFICES, DOMESTIC

Fig 2.1 A document reference

1 *Control number*. Each document has a unique number so that it can be easily identified.
2 *Title*.
3 *Author*.
4 *Source*. This tells us where the document came from, and usually includes such details as name of publisher, date of publication, and page references.
5 *Keywords*. These words tell us what the document is about.

A collection of references can be seen in Fig. 2.2. Try this exercise. See how many useful references you can find for an essay on industry as a source of air pollution. You have 60 seconds to complete the task.

How did you set about selecting references? You probably looked for all of those references containing the words pollution AND air AND industry. If you did, you performed what is called a logical operation. AND is used as a *logical operator*.

ONLINE

A computer can be programmed to perform the AND logical operation. Online is such a program. As well as searching on the keywords, Online allows searches of other fields. All of the data about one document is called a **computer record**. Each record has a number of distinct parts called **fields**. An Online record has 5 fields (Fig. 2.1). Each keyword can be regarded as a sub-field. The number of keywords varies from record to record. More keywords are required to describe the content of some documents than others. Because of this, Online records can be described as **variable-length records**. A collection of document records is called a **database**.

A retrieval system which deals with references to documents is called a *bibliographic information retrieval system*.

The Online search options are shown in Fig. 2.3. They are presented as a *menu*. When you select a menu number, you are telling the computer how you intend to search. If you select menu option 2, you are saying that you want to look in the title field of the records.

1

Pollution of rivers and lakes

Jones T

Pollution Review, Jan 1982, 60–66

POLLUTION, WATER, RIVERS, LAKES, SEWAGE, WASTE, DOMESTIC, INDUSTRY, CONTROL

2

Killing our rivers

Brown F

Pollution Journal, Jan 1982, 14–20

POLLUTION, WATER, RIVERS, SEWAGE, WASTE, EFFECTS, FISH

3

Future energy

Conrad M

Energy Times, Jan 1982, 24–29

ENERGY, POWER, ALTERNATIVE, SOLAR, WIND, TIDAL, WAVE, GEOTHERMAL

4

Pollution of the air

Pollock T

Pollution Review, Jan 1982, 30–33

POLLUTION, AIR, SMOG, EXHAUST, HEALTH

5

Air pollution

Kidder M

Pollution Journal, Jan 1982, 30–35

POLLUTION, AIR, SMOKE, CONTROL, LEGISLATION

6

Industry and pollution

Green N

Pollution Journal, Feb 1982, 55–59

POLLUTION, WATER, RIVERS, LAKES, INDUSTRY, CHEMICALS, FISH

7

Hydroelectric power

Simms P

Energy Times, Feb 1982, 48–56

ENERGY, POWER, STATIONS, DAMS, HYDROELECTRICITY, CONSTRUCTION

8

Pollution of the sea

Brown K

Pollution Review, Feb 1982, 60–67

POLLUTION, WATER, SEA, INDUSTRY, WASTE, OIL, CONTROL

9

Effects of air pollution

Wright L

Pollution Review, Feb 1982, 68–75

POLLUTION, AIR, SMOKE, DOMESTIC, INDUSTRY, CONTROL, LEGISLATION, EFFECTS

10

Introduction to air pollution

Want R

Pollution Review, Feb 1982, 63–67

POLLUTION, AIR, SMOKE, DOMESTIC, INDUSTRY, CONTROL, LEGISLATION

11

Air pollution

Vidal F

Pollution Journal, Feb 1982, 68–74

POLLUTION, AIR, SMOKE, MEASUREMENT, SULPHUR, DIOXIDE, LICHENS

12

Water power

Clagg J

Energy Times, Feb 1982, 71–79

ENERGY, POWER, HYDROELECTRICITY, TIDAL, WAVE

13

Energy from the sun

Koch A

Energy Times, Feb 1982, 80–88

ENERGY, POWER, SOLAR, COST, JAPAN, EFFICIENCY, OFFICES, DOMESTIC

14

Polluting water

Smith C

Pollution Review, Mar 1982, 80–83

POLLUTION, WATER, RIVERS, LAKES, CONTROL

15

Pollution: the Trent

Jackson E

Pollution Review, Mar 1982, 90–98

POLLUTION, WATER, RIVERS, TRENT, INDUSTRY, AGRICULTURE, WASTE, PESTICIDES, SEWAGE

16

British air pollution figures

Jackson K

Pollution Journal, Mar 1982, 75–83

POLLUTION, AIR, UK, SMOKE, SULPHUR, DIOXIDE, SULPHURIC, ACID, SURVEY, STATISTICS, LEGISLATION, CONTROL

17

Stretching our resources

Williams D

Science Journal, Mar 1982, 95–100

RECYCLING, WASTE, PAPER

18

Waste handling

Gluman C

Environmental Times, Mar 1982, 60–63

WASTE, REFUSE, DISPOSAL, SEPARATION, RECYCLING, UK, FRANCE

19

Offshore menace

Clarke C

Science Journal, Mar 1982, 90–94

POLLUTION, WATER, SEA, OIL

20

Industrial waste

Botham P

Pollution Review, Apr 1982, 126–132

POLLUTION, WATER, RIVERS, INDUSTRY, CONTROL

21

Domestic waste

Gibson F

Pollution Journal, Apr 1982, 90–96

POLLUTION, WASTE, REFUSE, DOMESTIC, RECYCLING, FRANCE

22

Nuclear power

Timms D

Energy Times, Apr 1982, 100–106

ENERGY, POWER, NUCLEAR, URANIUM, PLUTONIUM, WASTE

23

Technology and fuel prices

Jackson P

Energy Times, Apr 1982, 100–106

ENERGY, NUCLEAR, SOLAR, POWER, COST, EFFICIENCY

24

Home sweet home

Green N

Energy Times, Apr 1982, 107–110

ENERGY, DOMESTIC, SOLAR, POWER, WIND, METHANE, ALTERNATIVE, SELF-SUFFICIENCY

Fig 2.2 A collection of document references

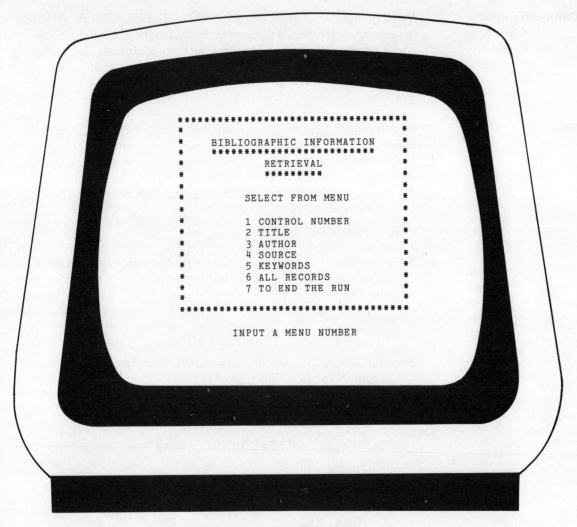

```
************************************
*                                  *
*   BIBLIOGRAPHIC INFORMATION       *
*   ***************************      *
*         RETRIEVAL                 *
*         *********                 *
*                                  *
*   SELECT FROM MENU                *
*                                  *
*     1 CONTROL NUMBER              *
*     2 TITLE                       *
*     3 AUTHOR                      *
*     4 SOURCE                      *
*     5 KEYWORDS                    *
*     6 ALL RECORDS                 *
*     7 TO END THE RUN              *
*                                  *
************************************

      INPUT  A  MENU  NUMBER
```

Fig 2.3   Screen display of the Online menu

Control number

Menu number 1 causes the prompt INPUT THE CONTROL NUMBER to appear. There are 24 document records in the Online database. These can be retrieved by inputting the control number. Try retrieving the records with control numbers 5 and 8. What are the titles on these document records?

Title

Menu number 2 causes the prompt INPUT THE TITLE to appear. There are three possible responses. Experiment with each one, noting the control numbers of document records found in each case.

1 *Input a complete title* All document records containing that title will be output. Try

   a `AIR POLLUTION`

2 *Input the left-hand part of a title* The computer will retrieve all document records with titles beginning with the combination of letters keyed in. Try

   a `AIR`
   b `HYDRO`

3 *Input a word* that you know or hope is embedded in the titles of document records. This type of search is communicated to the computer by inputting

   `SUB$`=Search term

   For example `SUB$=POLLUT`

   Experiment with

   a `SUB$=RIVERS`
   b `SUB$=TRENT`
   c `SUB$=TRE`

   There must be no spaces between the $, the comma and the first letter of the search term.

   Why might it be useful to be able to search for titles containing a particular word?

Author

Menu number 3 causes the prompt INPUT THE AUTHOR to appear. Either the whole author name or a left-hand segment may be input. Experiment by searching for records containing the following names or truncated name. Note the control numbers of records found in each case.

   a `JACKSON E`
   b `JACKSON`

   c The author name in one of the records is CLAG J, or is it
     CLAGG J? Perform a search to find the record whichever way it
     is spelt.

Source

Menu number 4 causes the prompt INPUT THE SOURCE to appear.
Either the whole source, including date of publication and page
numbers, or a left-hand segment may be input. Experiment with the
following, and note the control numbers found in each case.

```
a  POLLUTION REVIEW
b  POLLUTION REVIEW.MAR82
```

Keywords

Document records can be retrieved by a single keyword or
combination of keywords. Menu number 5 causes a second menu to
be displayed.

These are the logic options: AND, OR and NOT. Whichever you
select, the computer will explain how to proceed.

AND allows a search for document records containing, for example,
     term 1 AND term 2 AND term 3
where "term" is the word to be searched for.

OR allows a search for document records containing, for example,
     term 1 OR term 2 OR term 3

NOT allows a search for document records containing
     term 1 but NOT term 2.

Keyword searches using logical operators are considered in detail
on pages 32 and 33.

   To run a single-term search:

1 Select the KEYWORD option from the front page menu.
2 Select AND logic from the logic option menu.
3 Input the search term in response to the input prompt.
4 Input RUN in response to the next input prompt.

What are the control numbers of records containing the term FISH?

All records

Menu number 6 causes all of the records in the database to be output
in record order.

Stop

The command STOP causes the menu to be displayed. This command can be used:

- In response to an invitation to input a control number, title, author or source.
- In response to a prompt to input a keyword during a logical operation.
- Instead of pressing RETURN to continue after any record has been output.

NOTE   Some input does not require the use of the RETURN key, for example

- When selecting a menu number.
- When selecting a Logic Option menu number.

Keyword search using AND

Experiment with the following searches, noting the number of hits (records retrieved) in each case:

a `POLLUTION`
b `POLLUTION AND AIR`
c `POLLUTION AND AIR AND INDUSTRY`

What is the effect of the AND logical operator? Does it:
 i) increase the number of references?
 ii) decrease the number of references?
 iii) have no effect?

Does it do this
 i) usually?
 ii) sometimes?
 iii) never?

Read the screen instructions CAREFULLY.

Keyword search using OR

Experiment with the following searches, noting the number of hits in each case:

a `SOLAR`
b `WAVE`
c `SOLAR OR WAVE`
d `AIR`
e `WATER`
f `AIR OR WATER`

What is the effect of the OR logical operator? Does it:
 i) increase the number of references?
 ii) decrease the number of references?
 iii) have no effect?

Does it do this
 i) usually?
 ii) sometimes?
 iii) never?

Keyword search using NOT

Experiment with the following searches, noting the number of hits in each case:

a WASTE
b RECYCLING
c WASTE NOT RECYCLING
d NUCLEAR
e WASTE NOT NUCLEAR

What is the effect of the NOT logical operator? Does it:
  i) increase the number of references?
  ii) decrease the number of references?
  iii) have no effect?
Does it do this
  i) usually?
  ii) sometimes?
  iii) never?
The NOT logical operator often leads to problems in online searching. Examine the record with control number 23. Why would SOLAR NOT NUCLEAR be an unfortunate search for someone wanting references to documents about solar energy?

Input option summary

Field	Menu number	Input option
Control number	1	Whole number
Title	2	Whole title *or* Left-hand segment *or* SUB$ = substring
Author	3	Whole name. SURNAME INITIAL (with no punctuation) *or* Left-hand segment
Source	4	Whole source *or* Left-hand segment
Keywords	5	Second menu: 1 AND Logic 2 OR Logic 3 NOT Logic
All records	6	
End run	7	

INDEXING One of the problems facing the user of a computer
database is choosing the right search term(s) to input. The computer
will only find a record if the search term matches a keyword exactly.
To overcome this problem an Authority List is often used. This is a list
of terms which can be used by both indexer and searcher.

Authority List

ACCIDENT	FAST	NATURAL
ALTERNATIVE	FORECAST	NON-RENEWABLE
ATOMIC	FISSION	NUCLEAR
AUTHORITY	FOSSIL	
	FUEL	OIL
BREEDER	FUSION	OPEN CAST
	FUTURE	
COAL		PANELS
CONSERVATION		PETROLEUM (use oil)
CONSUMPTION	GAS	PHOTOGRAPH
CONVERSION	GENERATOR	PIPELINE
CONVERTER	GEOTHERMAL	PLANNING
COST	GOVERNMENT	PLUTONIUM
CRISIS		POWER
CRUDE	HAZARDS	
	HEAT	RESOURCES
DIAGRAM	HOMES (use domestic)	
DOMESTIC	HYDROELECTRICITY	SOLAR
DRILLING		STATION
	INDUSTRY	STATISTICS
EFFECT	INSULATION	
EFFICIENCY		TIDAL
ELECTRICITY	LEGISLATION	
ENERGY		WATER
EXCHANGE(R)	MINING	WAVE
EXPERIMENT		WIND
EXPLORATION		

1 Index the document entitled Energy Resources (which is a
passage taken from the book *Environmental Studies: a first
course* by Terry Jennings, published by Pitman Books). Make a
list of keywords using the authority list as a guide.

2 Consider whether there are any additional terms which you might
include in the keywords, which bring out the uniqueness of the
document.

Energy Resources

Most of our energy is derived from the combustion of **fossil fuels** such as coal, gas and oil. This store of energy was formed about 400 million years ago, or even earlier. When we burn fossil fuels, we are releasing energy that was trapped in the decayed forests or microscopic sea creatures of those ancient times. It is a disturbing fact that now, in a period of 12 months, we use up the energy that took about 400 000 years to accumulate in fossil fuels. It is impossible to replace these fuels, which means that eventually our store of fossil fuels will be empty. No-one can be certain about the size of the reserves. Coal is the most plentiful, and there should be enough to last two hundred years, even if we continue to use the fuel at the same rate as we do at the moment. In addition, coal has the advantage that it is found all over the world, from Australia to the Arctic circle. Russia has the biggest store of coal, followed by North America, China and Western Europe.

Oil and gas, on the other hand, are found in only certain parts of the world where geological conditions are right. The large oilfields lie mostly in the Middle East, Russia, North America and Africa. There are also large deposits under the seas, including the North Sea. Again, no-one knows how much oil and gas is there to be exploited, but most experts believe that, at the present rate of use, world supplies of oil and gas will run out sometime during the next century.

As we have already seen, energy lies at the heart of human progress. One-third of all the world's daily use of energy goes into industry. Almost as much energy is used in homes for heating and lighting. Transport accounts for a further 20 per cent, indicating how much we have come to depend on cars, buses, trains, ships and aircraft. Again, however, this is not the case throughout the world. On average, in the United States, each person uses 330 times as much energy as someone living in Ethiopia, and 60 times as much as someone in India, where the population is far, far larger than in America.

Energy demands are almost certain to rise in the future. As far as the fossil fuels are concerned, there is plenty of scope for reducing waste by using all forms of energy more efficiently. In the long term, the best way to save the energy used in transport is to reduce the weight and drag of the vehicles. The car is a wasteful user of petrol in that only about 10 to 14 per cent of the energy in the fuel is actually used to turn the wheels. Diesel engines are much more efficient, turning 28 to 35 per cent of the energy in the fuel into a usable form. There is thus great scope for the improvement of petrol engines.

A number of countries are looking at possible alternatives to petrol as fuel. One promising substance is alcohol, produced by fermenting sugar cane and other vegetable matter, and then distilling off the alcohol. The waste product is used as a fertilizer. The Brazilian railway started up its first alcohol-powered locomotive in 1979, and the State steel factories will soon use a combination of petrol and alcohol. More than 6 million cars are already powered by gasohol – a mixture of 85 per cent petrol and 15 per cent alcohol, which is cooler, cleaner and more efficient than petrol on its own. The United States has begun to invest more time and money in gasohol research, although these alcohol fuels seem best suited to large developing countries, like Brazil, which can turn over large areas to producing the vegetable matter needed to make it. Methane, from animal dung, is another possible fuel being tried out in some countries.

Energy is used in the home, mainly for space heating (67 per cent), water heating (25 per cent), lighting (1 per cent), and cooking (7 per cent). The main possibilities for saving energy are in improving the efficiency of heat production and preventing the loss of heat by draught-proofing and effective insulation.

DATA COLLECTION A computer record has a structure which must be kept to rigidly. To ensure that all of the data is collected and organised properly, it is necessary to use a Data Collection Sheet.

Design a Data Collection Sheet for an Online record, observing the following:

1 *Field Length*
 a Control number – 35 characters
 b Title   – 35 characters
 c Author   – 35 characters
 d Source   – 35 characters
 e Keywords   – 140 characters
2 *Keywords*
There may be 4 output lines, each of 35 characters. This includes separating semi-colons (run the program and examine a record). The computer never breaks words.

A word which is too long to fit on the end of a line is printed on the next line. When data is collected, ensure that it will fit into the available screen display space. Any characters in addition to the 140 allocated will be lost at the output stage.
3 Author
This should be input as
  surname space initial
4 Source
The format is
  Title. Month. Year. Page reference
  `POLLUTION REVIEW.FEB.82.68-75`

DATA INPUT In Online, data is stored within the program. This is unusual, but convenient for the purpose of experimenting with a microcomputer system. Data is usually held on magnetic disks (see page 64).

Load Online and immediately enter the following record, exactly as it appears. Do not confuse zero with the character O, and press the RETURN key at the end of each line.

A single asterisk marks the end of a record.

```
6000 DATA 25
6010 DATA RUNNING OUT OF FUEL
6020 DATA WILLIAMS K
6030 DATA ENERGY TIMES.APR82.106-114
6040 DATA COAL,OIL,GAS,FUEL,CRISIS
6050 DATA ENERGY
6060 DATA *
```

Try to retrieve this document record using the search skills which you have developed.

BLAISE

The British Library offers an online information service called BLAISE. Users of the system interact directly with a computer to find references to documents. A wide range of bibliographic databases can be searched. BLAISE-LINE is based on a computer in Harlow in Essex. BLAISE-LINK uses a computer at the National Library of Medicine in Washington, USA.

The databases are updated regularly. The frequency varies from database to database, and may be once a week, once a month, or perhaps once a quarter.

All of the databases can be searched offline. This means that requests for information can be sent to the BLAISE service where staff will carry out the searches.

BLAISE databases use two standard record formats:

a Machine Readable Catalogue (MARC) records.
b Medline records (Fig. 2.5). The Medline records contain a large abstract of the document. (An abstract is a summary of the document's content.)

The significance of the example Medline record in Fig. 2.5 is its sheer size. Over 4 million of these are available online.

Output identifiers, on the left-hand side, are used to tell the user what each part of the record is. The first three (AU, TI, LA) mean author, title and language of publication. MH means Mesh Heading. Theses are words and phrases which are used to index the document and can be likened to the keywords in the Online document records. The terms are selected from a list available to searcher and indexer.

AB means abstract. SO is the source.

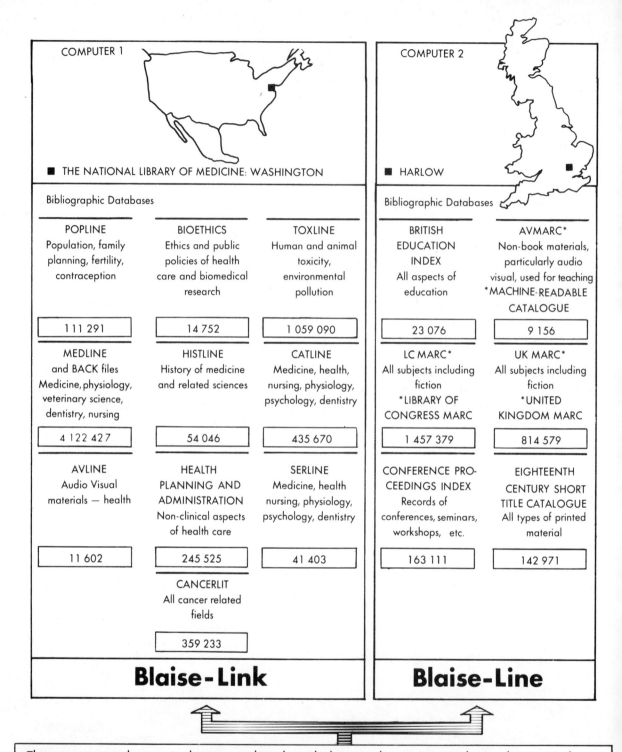

COMPUTER 1

■ THE NATIONAL LIBRARY OF MEDICINE: WASHINGTON

Bibliographic Databases

POPLINE	BIOETHICS	TOXLINE
Population, family planning, fertility, contraception	Ethics and public policies of health care and biomedical research	Human and animal toxicity, environmental pollution
111 291	14 752	1 059 090

MEDLINE	HISTLINE	CATLINE
and BACK files Medicine, physiology, veterinary science, dentistry, nursing	History of medicine and related sciences	Medicine, health, nursing, physiology, psychology, dentistry
4 122 427	54 046	435 670

AVLINE	HEALTH PLANNING AND ADMINISTRATION	SERLINE
Audio Visual materials — health	Non-clinical aspects of health care	Medicine, health nursing, physiology, psychology, dentistry
11 602	245 525	41 403

CANCERLIT
All cancer related fields

359 233

Blaise-Link

COMPUTER 2

■ HARLOW

Bibliographic Databases

BRITISH EDUCATION INDEX	AVMARC*
All aspects of education	Non-book materials, particularly audio visual, used for teaching *MACHINE-READABLE CATALOGUE
23 076	9 156

LC MARC*	UK MARC*
All subjects including fiction *LIBRARY OF CONGRESS MARC	All subjects including fiction *UNITED KINGDOM MARC
1 457 379	814 579

CONFERENCE PRO-CEEDINGS INDEX	EIGHTEENTH CENTURY SHORT TITLE CATALOGUE
Records of conferences, seminars, workshops, etc.	All types of printed material
163 111	142 971

Blaise-Line

The operator at the terminal interacts directly with the search program and can obtain an almost instant response to queries — searches for references. A search can be modified in the light of what the computer finds. (The figures quoted represent the number of records on line in June 1983)

Fig 2.4 The BLAISE system

```
AU - HENDERSON J
TI - EXORCISM AND POSSESSION IN PSYCHOTHERAPY PRACTICE
LA - ENG
MH - ADULT
MH - CASE REPORT
MH - FANTASY
MH - FEMALE
MH - HUMAN
MH - INFANT
MH - MALE
MH - MENTAL DISORDERS/*PSYCHOLOGY
MH - MOTHER-CHILD RELATIONS
MH - NEUROTIC DISORDERS/PSYCHOLOGY
MH - OBJECT ATTACHMENT
MH - PSYCHOANALYTIC THEORY
MH - PSYCHOTHERAPY/*METHODS
MH - PUBLIC OPINION
MH - *SPIRITUALISM
MH - STRESS: PSYCHOLOGICAL/PSYCHOLOGY
DA - 820614
DP - 1982 MAR
IS - 0706-7437
TA - CAN J PSYCHIATRY
UI - 82162349
PO - 129-34
SB - M
ZN - 21:107:567:176
IP - 2
UI - 27
JC - CLR
AA - AUTHOR
EM - 8208
AB - THERE HAS BEEN AN EVOLUTION IN THE LAYMAN'S CONCEPT OF MENTAL
     DISORDER. MEDIEVAL BELIEF IN POSSESSION BY DEMONS AND WITCHES
     GAVE WAY TO A 19TH CENTURY MEDICAL MODEL AND MORE RECENTLY
     CLASSICAL PSYCHOANALYTIC FORMULATIONS. CONCURRENTLY PROFESSIONAL
     HELPING ENDEAVOUR HAS MOVED INCREASINGLY FROM A MORE TRADITIONALLY
     MEDICAL TO PSYCHOTHERAPEUTIC PROCESS: AND FROM A CLASSICAL
     PSYCHOTHERAPEUTIC PROCESS WHEREIN THE THERAPIST REMAINED TO A
     DEGREE UNRESPONSIVE AND DETACHED TO A MORE MODERN EMPHASIS ON
     SUCH QUALITIES AS EMPATHY: SENSITIVITY: RELIABILITY: AND OPTIMISM
     AS INGREDIENTS OF SUCCESSFUL PSYCHOTHERAPEUTIC PRACTICE. FREUD'S
     ACCOUNT OF HAIZMANN'S DEMONOLOGICAL NEUROSIS USEFULLY FORMULATES
     THE POSSESSION CONCEPT IN PSYCHOLOGICAL TERMS. HOWEVER, RECENT
     DEVELOPMENTS IN PSYCHOTHERAPEUTIC PRACTICE ARGUE FOR A VALIDITY
     IN THE POSSESSION MODEL OF PSYCHOLOGICAL DISTRESS. THE POSSESSING
     FORCES OF OBJECT RELATIONS PSYCHOLOGY ARE OF COURSE NOT THE
     POSSESSING DEMONS AND WITCHES OF MEDIEVAL TIMES BUT THE
     POSSESSING GOOD AND BAD OBJECTS OF EARLY INTRAPSYCHIC LIFE SET UP
     THROUGH PROCESSES OF INTROJECTION AND INCORPORATION IN RESPONSE
     TO FRUSTRATION IN THE EARLY INFANT-MOTHER RELATIONSHIP. POINTS OF
     SIMILARITY IN THIS COMPARISON SHOULD NOT OBSCURE FEATURES OF
     CONTRAST--THERE IS NO PLACE FOR HISTRIONIC MANIPULATION NOR FOR A
     MORALISTIC ATTITUDE IN THE PRACTICE OF PSYCHOTHERAPY. A CASE IS
     DESCRIBED TO ILLUSTRATE THESE POINTS.
80 - CAN J PSYCHIATRY 1982 MAR 27(2):129-34
```

Fig 2.5 A typical Medline record

3 AIRLINE

Most airlines use computers to achieve efficient booking of flights. When seats are booked, data concerning timetables and prices needs to be consulted, and the customers must be informed of the seats available so that they can make a choice. To complicate matters, flights may be booked worldwide. That is, seats on a flight from London to New York may be booked from an office in Rome.

How can an airline make seats available to travellers across the world without booking the same seat twice and without being left with unsold seats? The answer is that they use a **real-time computer system**. Each airline office has terminals linked by telephone to a central computer. This means that they can obtain up-to-date information on seat sales and that booking details can be updated immediately

seats are sold. Since the computer can process sales rapidly, any new customer is offered an accurate choice of seats, wherever the booking is made.

Some extracts from a recent British Airways Worldwide timetable are shown in Fig. 3.1. They give details of flights between London and three cities: Paris, Amsterdam and Brussels. How much information is given? What do the numbers and abbreviations tell you? What types of aircraft are used?

The complete timetable has over 100 pages of flight details; those shown here represent about 3 pages. Information is also given about airports, worldwide booking offices, aircraft types, and other airlines which appear in the timetable.

Fig 3.1 British Airways timetable

40

London ► Paris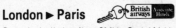

Depart London, Heathrow Airport, BA flights: Terminal 1 (minimum check-in time at pier gate 20 mins)
Other flights: Terminal 2 (minimum check-in time 25 mins)
Reservations tel 01 3705411

16 May – 22 Oct	Daily	**0640**	**0840(a)**	non-stop	**BA302**	TRD/757
16 May – 22 Oct	MoTuWeThFrSa	0730	0930(a)	non-stop	AF807	AB3
16 May – 22 Oct	Daily	**0830**	**1030(a)**	non-stop	**BA304**	L10/757
16 May – 22 Oct	Daily	0930	1130(a)	non-stop	AF809	AB3
16 May – 22 Oct	Daily	**1030**	**1230(a)**	non-stop	**BA306**	L10/757
16 May – 22 Oct	Daily	1130	1330(a)	non-stop	AF811	AB3
16 May – 21 Oct	MoTuWeThFr	**1230**	**1430(a)**	non-stop	**BA308**	TRD
16 May – 22 Oct	Daily	1330	1530(a)	non-stop	AF813	AB3/727
16 May – 22 Oct	Daily	**1430**	**1630(a)**	non-stop	**BA312**	L10/757
16 May – 22 Oct	Daily	1530	1730(a)	non-stop	AF815	AB3
16 May – 22 Oct	Daily	**1645**	**1845(a)**	non-stop	**BA314**	L10/757
16 May – 22 Oct	Daily	1730	1930(a)	non-stop	AF817	AB3/727
16 May – 22 Oct	Daily	**1845**	**2045(a)**	non-stop	**BA316**	L10/TRD
16 May – 22 Oct	Daily	1930	2130(a)	non-stop	AF819	AB3
16 May – 22 Oct	Daily	2030	2230(a)	non-stop	AF821	727

Paris ► London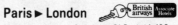

Depart Paris, Charles de Gaulle Airport, BA Terminal 1, AF Terminal 2
(minimum acceptance time for baggage 25 mins)
(minimum check-in for passengers 15 mins at the Satellite gate)
Reservations tel 17781414

16 May – 22 Oct	MoTuWeThFrSa	0830(a)	0830	non-stop	AF808	AB3
16 May – 22 Oct	Daily	0910(a)	0910	non-stop	AF806	727
16 May – 22 Oct	Daily	**0930(a)**	**0930**	non-stop	**BA303**	TRD/757
16 May – 22 Oct	Daily	1030(a)	1030	non-stop	AF810	AB3
16 May – 22 Oct	Daily	**1130(a)**	**1130**	non-stop	**BA305**	L10/757
16 May – 22 Oct	Daily	1230(a)	1230	non-stop	AF812	AB3/727
16 May – 22 Oct	Daily	**1330(a)**	**1330**	non-stop	**BA307**	L10/757
16 May – 22 Oct	Daily	1430(a)	1430	non-stop	AF814	AB3
16 May – 21 Oct	MoTuWeThFr	**1530(a)**	**1530**	non-stop	**BA309**	TRD
16 May – 22 Oct	Daily	1630(a)	1630	non-stop	AF816	AB3/727
16 May – 22 Oct	Daily	**1730(a)**	**1730**	non-stop	**BA313**	L10/757
16 May – 22 Oct	Daily	1830(a)	1830	non-stop	AF818	AB3
16 May – 22 Oct	Daily	**1945(a)**	**1945**	non-stop	**BA315**	L10/757
16 May – 22 Oct	Daily	2030(a)	2030	non-stop	AF820	AB3
16 May – 22 Oct	Daily	**2145(a)**	**2145**	non-stop	**BA317**	L10/TRD

London ► Amsterdam

Depart London, Heathrow Airport, BA flights: Terminal 1 (minimum check-in time at pier gate 20 mins)
Other flights: Terminal 2 (minimum check-in time 30 mins)
Reservations tel 01 3705411

16 May – 22 Oct	Daily	**0815**	**1015(a)**	non-stop	**BA406**	TRD
16 May – 22 Oct	Daily	0900	1100(a)	non-stop	KL116	DC8
16 May – 22 Oct	Daily	**1015**	**1215(a)**	non-stop	**BA408**	TRD
16 May – 22 Oct	Daily	1100	1300(a)	non-stop	KL118	DC8/DC9
16 May – 22 Oct	Daily	1300	1500(a)	non-stop	KL120	DC9
16 May – 22 Oct	Daily	**1415**	**1615(a)**	non-stop	**BA414**	TRD
16 May – 22 Oct	Daily	1500	1700(a)	non-stop	KL122	DC8
16 May – 22 Oct	Daily	**1615**	**1815(a)**	non-stop	**BA416**	TRD
16 May – 22 Oct	Daily	1700	1900(a)	non-stop	KL124	DC9
16 May – 21 Oct	MoTuWeThFrSu	**1815**	**2015(a)**	non-stop	**BA418**	TRD
16 May – 22 Oct	Daily	1900	2100(a)	non-stop	KL126	DC8/DC9
16 May – 21 Oct	MoTuWeThFrSu	**2030**	**2230(a)**	non-stop	**BA422**	TRD

Amsterdam ► London

Depart Amsterdam Airport (minimum check-in time 30 mins)

Reservations tel 229333

16 May – 22 Oct	Daily	0800(a)	0800	non-stop	KL115	DC8
16 May – 22 Oct	MoTuWeThFrSa	**0845(a)**	**0845**	non-stop	**BA401**	TRD
16 May – 22 Oct	Daily	1000(a)	1000	non-stop	KL117	DC8/DC9
16 May – 22 Oct	Daily	**1100(a)**	**1100**	non-stop	**BA407**	TRD
16 May – 22 Oct	Daily	1200(a)	1200	non-stop	KL119	DC9
16 May – 22 Oct	Daily	**1300(a)**	**1300**	non-stop	**BA409**	TRD
16 May – 22 Oct	Daily	1400(a)	1400	non-stop	KL121	DC8
16 May – 22 Oct	Daily	1600(a)	1600	non-stop	KL123	DC9
16 May – 22 Oct	Daily	**1700(a)**	**1700**	non-stop	**BA415**	TRD
16 May – 22 Oct	Daily	1800(a)	1800	non-stop	KL125	DC8/DC9
16 May – 22 Oct	Daily	**1900(a)**	**1900**	non-stop	**BA417**	TRD
16 May – 21 Oct	MoTuWeThFrSu	**2100(a)**	**2100**	non-stop	**BA419**	TRD

London ► Brussels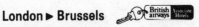

Depart London, Heathrow Airport, BA flights: Terminal 1 (minimum check-in time at pier gate 20 mins)
Other flights: Terminal 2 (minimum check-in time 35 mins)
Reservations tel 01 3705411

16 May – 21 Oct	MoTuWeThFr	**0805**	**1000(a)**	non-stop	**BA374**	B11
16 May – 24 Sep	Daily	0845	1040	non-stop	SN602	73S
25 Sep – 22 Oct	Daily	0945	1040	non-stop	SN602	73S
16 May – 22 Oct	Daily	**1005**	**1200(a)**	non-stop	**BA376**	B11
16 May – 30 Jun	MoTuWeThFr	1045	1240	non-stop	SN604	73S
1 Sep – 23 Sep	MoTuWeThFr	1045	1240	non-stop	SN604	73S
26 Sep – 21 Oct	MoTuWeThFr	1145	1240	non-stop	SN604	73S
16 May – 21 Oct	MoTuWeThFr	**1205**	**1400(a)**	non-stop	**BA378**	EQV
16 May – 24 Sep	Daily	1445	1640	non-stop	SN606	73S
25 Sep – 22 Oct	Daily	1545	1640	non-stop	SN606	73S
16 May – 22 Oct	Daily	**1605**	**1800(a)**	non-stop	**BA384**	73S/TRD
16 May – 24 Sep	Daily	1645	1840	non-stop	SN608	73S
25 Sep – 22 Oct	Daily	1745	1840	non-stop	SN608	73S
16 May – 24 Sep	Daily	1845	2040	non-stop	SN610	73S
16 May – 21 Oct	MoTuWeThFrSu	**1905**	**2100(a)**	non-stop	**BA388**	73S
25 Sep – 22 Oct	Daily	1945	2040	non-stop	SN610	73S
16 May – 23 Sep	MoTuWeThFr	2030	2225	non-stop	SN612	73S
26 Sep – 21 Oct	MoTuWeThFr	2130	2225	non-stop	SN612	73S
16 May – 16 Oct	Su	2130	2325(a)	non-stop	SN614	73S

Brussels ► London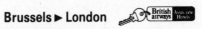

Depart Brussels, National Airport (minimum check-in time 30 mins)

Reservations tel 022194220/027519699

16 May – 24 Sep	Daily	0745	0745	non-stop	SN601	73S
25 Sep – 22 Oct	Daily	0745	0845	non-stop	SN601	73S
16 May – 22 Oct	MoTuWeThFrSa	**0845(a)**	**0845**	non-stop	**BA373**	73S
16 May – 30 Jun	MoTuWeThFr	0955	0955	non-stop	SN603	73S
1 Sep – 23 Sep	MoTuWeThFr	0955	0955	non-stop	SN603	73S
26 Sep – 21 Oct	MoTuWeThFr	0955	1055	non-stop	SN603	73S
16 May – 21 Oct	MoTuWeThFr	**1045(a)**	**1045**	non-stop	**BA375**	B11
16 May – 22 Oct	Daily	**1245(a)**	**1245**	non-stop	**BA377**	B11
16 May – 24 Sep	Daily	1345	1345	non-stop	SN605	73S
25 Sep – 22 Oct	Daily	1345	1445	non-stop	SN605	73S
16 May – 21 Oct	MoTuWeThFr	**1445(a)**	**1445**	non-stop	**BA379**	EQV
16 May – 20 May	Daily	1545	1545	non-stop	SN607	73S
22 May – 23 Sep	MoTuWeThFrSu	1545	1545	non-stop	SN607	73S
25 Sep – 22 Oct	Daily	1545	1645	non-stop	SN607	73S
16 May – 24 Sep	Daily	1745	1745	non-stop	SN609	73S
25 Sep – 22 Oct	Daily	1745	1845	non-stop	SN609	73S
16 May – 22 Oct	Daily	**1845(a)**	**1845**	non-stop	**BA385**	73S/TRD
16 May – 23 Sep	MoTuWeThFr	1945	1945	non-stop	SN611	73S
26 Sep – 21 Oct	MoTuWeThFr	1945	2045	non-stop	SN611	73S
16 May – 16 Oct	Su	2045(a)	2045	non-stop	SN613	73S

SwiftAir

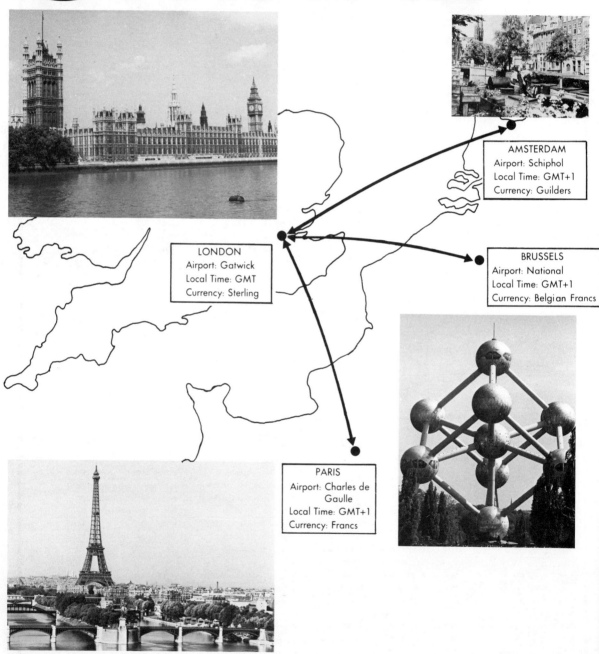

AMSTERDAM
Airport: Schiphol
Local Time: GMT+1
Currency: Guilders

LONDON
Airport: Gatwick
Local Time: GMT
Currency: Sterling

BRUSSELS
Airport: National
Local Time: GMT+1
Currency: Belgian Francs

PARIS
Airport: Charles de Gaulle
Local Time: GMT+1
Currency: Francs

An airline, SwiftAir, issues timetables giving details of flights between different airports. SwiftAir operates on routes between London and the cities of Paris, Amsterdam and Brussels. The daily flights are shown in the timetables in Fig. 3.3 (pages 44 and 45).

Local times are used, which means that, for example, you can leave Paris at 0800 and arrive in London at 0755 (table D).

Using the timetables

1 Suppose that you wished to travel from London to Brussels.
   a Which table would you use to select a flight?
   b If you wanted to arrive by 4.00 pm (1600 hrs) which flights would be suitable?

2 A businessman in Paris has a meeting arranged for midday in London and an early evening meeting in Amsterdam. Which flights and times would be suitable?

Booking an airline seat

Booking a seat on a flight involves searching the Airline's timetables to find times which are suitable.

DESTINATION   Imagine that you are planning a flight on a particular day, say 8 December. Decide at what time during the day you would like to make your flight, and choose a departure and destination city.

BOOKING   Copy the booking form (Fig. 3.2) into your exercise book or use one supplied by your teacher. Fill in the details of your chosen flight.

Fig 3.2   SwiftAir booking form

SwiftAir BOOKING FORM	
DATE	8th December
DEPARTURE	
DESTINATION	
DEPARTURE TIME (APPROX)	
NUMBER OF SEATS	
NAME	

All times are local   B11 = BAC 1–11   Y = ECONOMY

Table A LONDON–PARIS

Flight number Aircraft Class	SWA 001 B 11 Y	SWA 002 B 11 Y	SWA 003 B 11 Y	SWA 004 B 11 Y	SWA 005 B 11 Y
LONDON dep (Gatwick)	0730	1130	1330	1530	1930
PARIS arr (Charles de Gaulle)	0925	1325	1525	1725	2125

Table B LONDON–AMSTERDAM

Flight number Aircraft Class	SWA 006 B 11 Y	SWA 007 B 11 Y	SWA 008 B 11 Y
LONDON dep (Gatwick)	0745	1315	1945
AMSTERDAM arr (Schiphol)	0940	1510	2140

Table C LONDON–BRUSSELS

Flight number Aircraft Class	SWA 009 B 11 Y	SWA 010 B 11 Y	SWA 011 B 11 Y
LONDON dep (Gatwick)	0755	1155	1925
BRUSSELS arr (National)	0950	1350	2120

MANUAL LOOK-UP   Study the timetables (Fig.3.3). Find the correct table and then look for flights to suit your requirements. Remember to look for times around the one you have chosen in order to find a number of possibilities, if you can.

Fig 3.3 SwiftAir timetable

Table D PARIS–LONDON

Flight number	SWA 012	SWA 013	SWA 014	SWA 015	SWA 016
Aircraft	B 11	B 11	B 11	B 11	B 11
Class	Y	Y	Y	Y	Y
PARIS dep (Charles de Gaulle)	0800	1200	1600	1800	2200
LONDON arr (Gatwick)	0755	1155	1555	1755	2155

Table E AMSTERDAM–LONDON

Flight number	SWA 017	SWA 018	SWA 019
Aircraft	B 11	B 11	B 11
Class	Y	Y	Y
AMSTERDAM dep (Schiphol)	0815	1415	1915
LONDON arr (Gatwick)	0815	1415	1915

Table F BRUSSELS–LONDON

Flight number	SWA 020	SWA 021	SWA 022
Aircraft	B 11	B 11	B 11
Class	Y	Y	Y
BRUSSELS dep (National)	0800	1605	2150
LONDON arr (Gatwick)	0755	1600	2145

Finding a suitable flight in a busy airline schedule can be a very time-consuming task, and it can be made even more complicated if there are not many seats available. Then the search would have to be repeated until seats are found. Sometimes it is useful to have a list of possible flights to choose from.

COMPUTER SEARCH   SwiftAir has a computerised passenger booking service. You are invited to use this service for your flight. Take the completed booking form to a booking operator, who will input your request and obtain details of the booking situation (or simply key it in yourself). You must then make your choice of flights, or not – if the time of an available flight does not suit you. The computer will prompt the operator by printing questions on the screen. Each question will need data typed in from your booking form. Finally, you will have to choose from the flights available. The complete sequence might appear as shown in Fig. 3.4.

THE BOOKING SYSTEM   When the program is running, a menu of options is presented. Data is input during the "Booking" sequence and the files can be interrogated for information in the "Passenger Check", "Daily Accounts", and "Seat Statistics" options. Type the option number you require. There is no need to press the RETURN key. (Typing EXIT at any stage will abandon an enquiry.) Some data has been included in the program file to begin with.

SEARCHING THE TIMETABLES   When a search is to be made of the timetables, what data is required? After each input the RETURN key must be pressed.

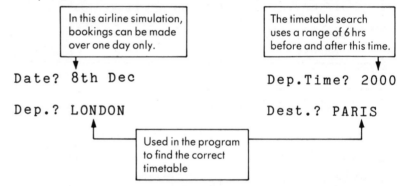

In this airline simulation, bookings can be made over one day only.		The timetable search uses a range of 6 hrs before and after this time.
Date? 8th Dec		Dep.Time? 2000
Dep.? LONDON	Used in the program to find the correct timetable	Dest.? PARIS

Some simple checks, or **validation**, of the data takes place on input. Only the airports listed can be used; they must be spelt correctly, and the time must be given in the correct format, the 24-hour format.

SCREEN INFORMATION   The details available in the timetable are presented only if any suitable flights are found

4	SWA004	1530	LONDON	PARIS
Timetable entry no.	Flight no.	Departure time	Departure	Destination

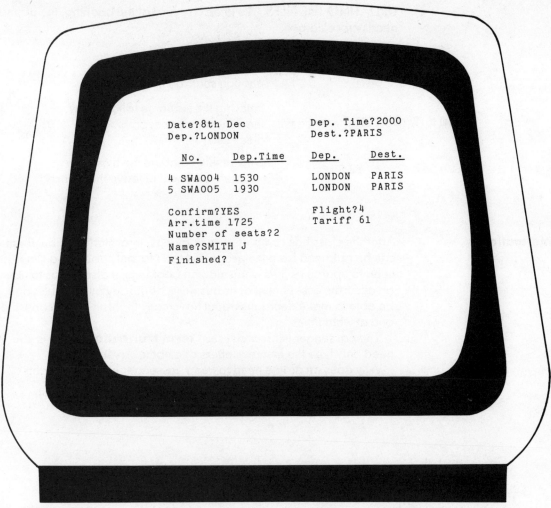

```
        Date?8th Dec          Dep. Time?2000
        Dep.?LONDON           Dest.?PARIS

          No.      Dep.Time    Dep.      Dest.

        4 SWA004   1530        LONDON    PARIS
        5 SWA005   1930        LONDON    PARIS

        Confirm?YES           Flight?4
        Arr.time 1725         Tariff 61
        Number of seats?2
        Name?SMITH J
        Finished?
```

Fig 3.4   Screen display of SwiftAir computer booking
system

How much of this information was given by the user? What other information might a real airline system provide?

After confirming that a booking is to be made, a flight is chosen by selecting the timetable entry number:

```
Confirm? YES                    Flight? 4
```

Two extra pieces of information are then given: the arrival time of the flight chosen and the tariff.

```
Arr.time 1725                   Tariff 61
```

UPDATING THE FILES   To keep a record of the booking, the airline needs more data:

```
Number of seats ? 2
```
← A check is made that there are enough seats on this flight.

```
Name ? SMITH J
```
← Entering the surname followed by the initials makes searching the files easier.

```
Finished ? YES
```
← Only at this point are the files updated. EXIT would leave them unchanged.

Information

After the class has completed its bookings, information about them can be obtained from the program files. Not only does an airline need to update its files when making bookings, it also needs to have an accurate assessment of its business, as quickly as possible, and to be able to make decisions about how many flights it should operate and at what times.

The passenger list search uses "**term truncation**", that is you need only type the first few letters of a name. Try it and see.

Why does an airline need to keep passenger lists for its flights?

British airways

Airlines have been using computer reservation systems since the mid-1960s. When British Airways was formed, by a merger of BEA and BOAC in 1972, two computer systems, BEACON and BOADICEA, were already in use. These two have since been superseded by BABS, a comprehensive reservation system, and other applications have been developed. The real-time systems include: hotel reservation, passenger check-in, fare quotations, cargo control, and flight planning.

British Airways real-time passenger services make use of a range of computer programs designed to assist with passenger handling. This begins with a customer enquiry about a seat on a flight and ends when passengers disembark on completion of their flight.

A worldwide airline needs communication links and British Airways has a network of high-speed data links and telegraph circuits covering 400 cities and airports. Passenger reservations are made by contacting British Airways offices, airports, or through other airline booking systems. The BABS operation at Heathrow Airport handles nearly 3000 terminals in 66 countries. British Airways flights, and those of other airlines as well, can be displayed so that customers can select flights. Seat reservations can be made immediately and cancelled seats become available quickly to other customers. It is also possible to make reservations for connecting flights and for hotels en route, as well as inter-airline bookings.

The real-time booking system makes it possible for cancelled seats to be available for immediate re-sale and this leads to improved booking efficiency. It is estimated that, for clerical work, staff costs have been reduced by about 30%. Airlines are keen to provide better customer service and develop passenger confidence, and computer systems have helped them to do this.

Passenger booking

When a passenger books a seat on a flight, a record is created on a booking file. The passenger name record contains details of the ticket, address and telephone number of the passenger, and any special requirements. The information is available at departure control as well as for sales analysis and emergencies. The passenger record file holds about one million records and about 40 000 bookings are made each day. It is intended that the booking system will develop so that fully automated booking, ticket production and accounting will be possible.

As passengers check in for their flights, booking details can be consulted for recorded reservations, or, indeed, new passenger details can be accepted. The on-the-spot updating of the file helps to ensure that as many seats as

Flight control

possible are sold. Around 200 passengers an hour are dealt with by departure control in the busiest summer periods. Inspection of the passenger lists enables an assessment of the cargo requirements to be made, and the computer calculates the weight and load distribution details for each flight. All passenger handling documents are produced automatically, and details are transmitted to any "stop-off points" during the flight.

Information for flight operations is also provided. Flight schedules are noted from the airline timetable system and up-to-date records of aircraft and crews are kept. The progress of flights already in operation is monitored to assist airport controllers. Weather forecasts are received directly from the Meteorological Office by computer data link, and flight plans are produced specifying flight tracks and fuel requirements.

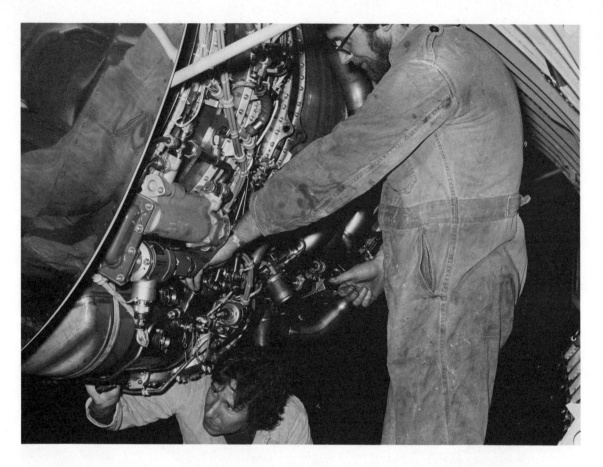

Aircraft maintenance

The aircraft need to be mantained regularly, and supplies of spare parts must be available. Data is collected for component control, aircraft overhaul planning, and engine logging. Computer analysis attempts to provide early warning of faults.

Cargo control

Airlines handle commercial cargo as well as passengers and their luggage. The progress of export cargo through the warehouse is monitored by the computer. Details necessary for warehouse and customs control are produced, and permanent records are kept on microfiche.

British Airways was involved in the development of LACES, a real-time system for import control, operated by the National Data Processing Service for Customs and Excise, airlines and freight agents.

Financial services

Commercial statistics are stored in the computer system for up to two years and are used as a database for market research and planning on tariffs reports. As well as payroll applications, the computer handles pension payments, pension fund investments, and general staff and pension records.

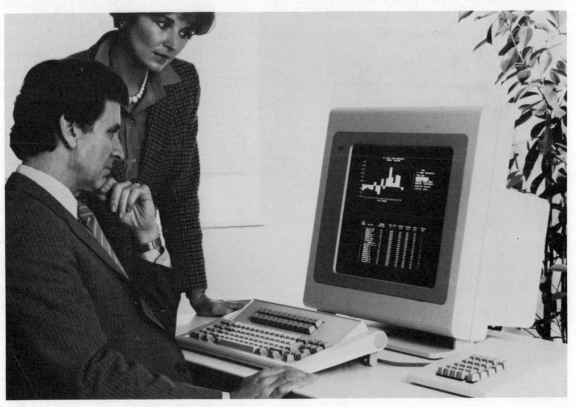

Hardware

Any real-time, mass-data system requires a large-capacity random-access store (see p. 64). This need is usually filled by using magnetic disk store. The British Airways computer centres use large-capacity central processors and they access data from a large number of disk storage devices. Staff involved in the computer operations total approximately 1600, of which 370 are concerned with data communications. An important feature of worldwide passenger seat reservations is the jointly owned international airline message switching network, which is operated by SITA (Societe Internationale de Telecommunications Aeronautiques).

There are three British Airways computer centres: Heathrow Airport, The West London Terminal, and Viscount House. Between them they operate an astounding array of hardware. Fig. 3.5 shows the range and quantity of hardware which they use.

The real-time systems, which use only part of this hardware, must be operational twenty four hours a day, seven days a week.

1 A method of booking seats, used before the computer was available, was to allocate blocks of seats to different booking offices. What are the disadvantages of such a system?
2 Airlines managed with manual booking systems in the past. What were the reasons for changing to computer booking?
3 The British Airways computer system uses a large number of disk units for backing store. Why is this so?
4 The booking system operates 7 days a week, 24 hours a day. How could such an operation be staffed? How do they cope in the event of breakdowns or cuts in the power supply?

Computer systems

All computer systems, whether large or small, have essentially the same four elements: device(s) to input data; a central processor to process data; device(s) to output information; and device(s) to store data and programs not in use.

CENTRAL PROCESSORS

Printers
13

8

Card Readers
7

Disk Devices
298

Magnetic Tape Drives
87

Fig 3.5 Hardware used in a large real-time system
(British Airways)

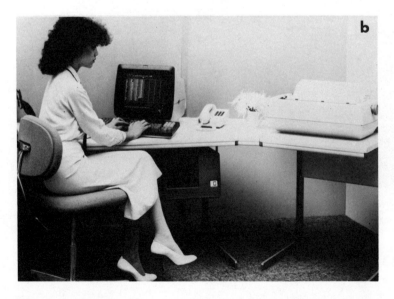

Fig 3.6 Microcomputer systems

a An ICL microcomputer system designed for use in a retail environment
b An ICL microcomputer-based word processor
c Apple's Lisa system
d A GEC microcomputer with 8-inch disk store unit

MICROCOMPUTERS Typical microcomputer systems have the following components (see Fig. 3.6):

1 A central processor unit – responsible for all of the data processing.
2 A keyboard – for inputting data.
3 A visual display screen – used to output information.

4 A printer – used to output information.
5 Floppy disks (backing store) – used to store data and programs not in use.
6 Disk drives – used to hold the floppy disks.

Cassette tapes and tape recorders can also be used to store data and programs not in use.

Fig 3.7   Mainframe systems

a   A Honeywell Information systems mainframe system
b   An IBM processor complex
c   General view of a Honeywell mainframe computer room showing banks of tape drives, disk pack drives, a line printer

MAINFRAME COMPUTERS   A mainframe computer system differs from a microcomputer system in processing capability. Mainframes can access large volumes of data and process that data very quickly. There are often other devices, called peripherals, linked to the computer which are used for input, output and storage of data. A microcomputer, by comparison, is slower, and it handles smaller quantities of data. Often, mainframe computers support a number of users, or have a number of programs running at the same time.

A typical mainframe system has the following components (see Fig. 3.7):

1   The central processor.
2   The operator's console – from here an operator has complete operational control over the computer.
3   A line printer.
4   Disk drive units.
5   Magnetic tape units.
6   Terminals – keyboard and visual display screen incorporated into a single unit.

Card readers and paper tape readers are also used for input.

THE CENTRAL PROCESSOR UNIT The CPU has three parts (see Fig. 3.8):

1 The **Arithmetic and Logic Unit (ALU)** This is where all computer arithmetic is performed. It is also used for logical operations and for comparing binary patterns.

2 The **Control Unit** This controls the step-by-step working of the computer, ensuring that data is passed from one part of the system to another as required. It ensures that the sequence of operations laid down in the program is carried out.

3 The **Central Memory** This is where programs are held while they are running. Data, input from the keyboard or some other device, or taken from the backing store, or created by the program, is also held in central memory while the program is in operation.

Fig 3.8 Outline of a computer system

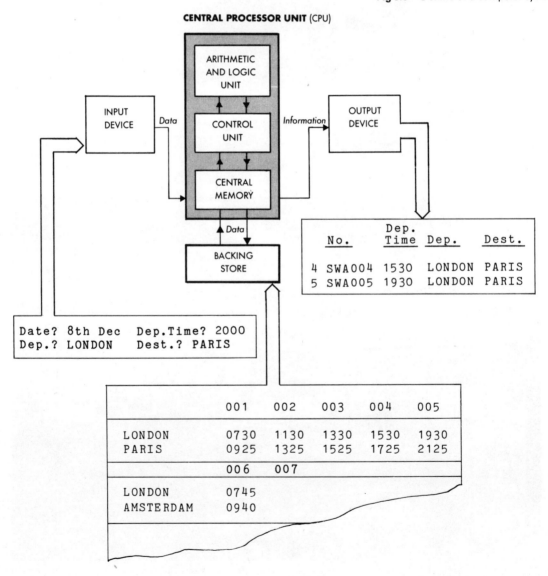

BACKING STORE The data in the central memory of a computer, in the central processor unit, needs to be accessed quickly. Inevitably, this means that main memory is an expensive item and it is also limited in its size (capacity). Large quantities of data can be held more cheaply, and permanently, as backing store. Thus a compromise is made between quantity and cheapness against speed of access. Usually, magnetic tape and magnetic disks provide the backing store; less commonly, nowadays, magnetic drums are used. In the future, other technologies, such as magnetic bubble memories, may become cheaper or more convenient alternatives.

Data in a computer is often coded by patterns of zeros and ones. For example, 01000001 might code the letter A. Each 0 and each 1 is called a binary digit, or **bit**. A group of bits coding one character is called a **byte**. Inside the central processor, electronic pulses represent the patterns of zeros and ones, but for tape and disk backing store, tiny magnetic areas are used instead. On magnetic tape, each coded pattern is recorded as one frame across the tape, but disks use circular tracks.

MAGNETIC TAPE Data is stored on reels of magnetic tape, like audio tape. Tape can be *written to* and *read from* when it is loaded on to a tape drive (Fig. 3.9).

The length and width of tape can vary but, typically, tapes are 2400 feet (732 metres) long and ½ inch wide. Such a tape can hold more than 30 million characters of data, depending on how densely the bits are packed, and reading and writing speeds can be in excess of 100 000 characters per second. The data is recorded in blocks with gaps between them (Fig. 3.10), and there are identification labels at the beginning of files.

A disadvantage of magnetic tape is that it might take several minutes to reach a particular piece of data at the other end of the tape, since the records follow one after the other along the tape. This kind of storage is referred to as **sequential**, or **serial**.

It is particularly useful for applications where the records can be processed sequentially, for example a payroll, where employee records might be in alphabetical order.

Microcomputers also use magnetic tape, but they use the cassette audio tapes suitable for conventional home tape recorders. Good-quality tape is necessary, and sometimes the cassette tape deck is built into the microcomputer.

Fig 3.9a   A reel of IBM data processing tape

Fig 3.9b   A cassette tape recorder

Fig 3.9*c* Magnetic tape reel-to reel drive: a GEC vertical configuration

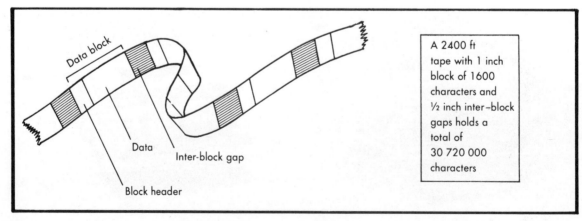

Data block

Data

Inter-block gap

Block header

A 2400 ft tape with 1 inch block of 1600 characters and ½ inch inter–block gaps holds a total of 30 720 000 characters

Fig 3.10 Data organisation on magnetic tape

Fig 3.9d   Magnetic tape reel-to-reel drive: an IBM
horizontal configuration

DISK STORE   Hard disks, which are about 2 feet (600 mm) in diameter, are available combined in packs on a common spindle or as a single disk in a protective cartridge (Fig. 3.11).

Common disk packs carry 6 or 11 disks. The upper side of the top disk and the lower side of the bottom disk usually act as a protective surface, so that 10 and 20 sides, respectively, are available for data storage. Interchangeable disk packs can be loaded onto a disk drive which rotates the disks at around 3000 revolutions per minute.

Data stored on a disk, or disk pack, can be accessed *directly*, regardless of its position, without the need to read other data on the disk. This is accomplished by keeping a record of the position (location) on the disk where data is stored. Direct access, or **random access** is very fast and, as a result, disks are often preferred to magnetic tape, although they are more expensive.

Read/write heads move in between the disks (Fig. 3.12), close to the magnetic surfaces, but

Fig 3.11   A GEC disk cartridge being loaded into its drive

without touching them. The rotation of the disks causes air turbulence (swirling) and this creates enough pressure to keep the heads from touching the surfaces. To allow this, the surface of the disk must not become contaminated. The packs are handled with a plastic cover which is detached only when the pack is loaded onto the drive, and filters keep out particles of dust. If a head crash occurs, and contact between the heads and disk surface is made, the magnetic surface and also the read/write heads can both be badly damaged.

Magnetic-coated disks, although they may vary in size, share the same system of organising the data. Data is stored on concentric *tracks* and each track is divided into a number of *sectors* (Fig. 3.13).

It is often convenient to group the corresponding tracks on each surface as a unit of storage, called a *cylinder* (Fig. 3.14), since the read/write heads can remain in one position while all the tracks are being accessed.

Fig 3.12 The principle of operation of a disk store

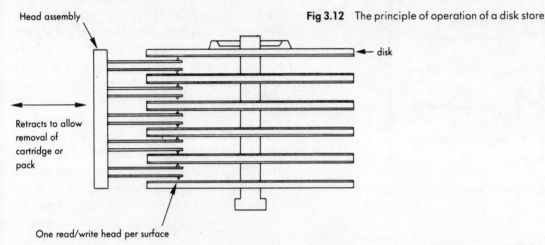

Head assembly

disk

Retracts to allow removal of cartridge or pack

One read/write head per surface

Fig 3.13 Data organisation on a magnetic disk

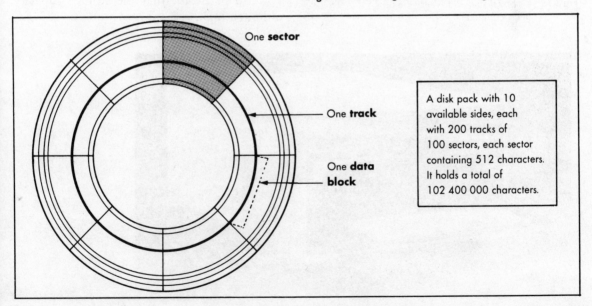

One **sector**

One **track**

One **data block**

A disk pack with 10 available sides, each with 200 tracks of 100 sectors, each sector containing 512 characters. It holds a total of 102 400 000 characters.

FLEXIBLE DISKS Floppy disks (Fig. 3.15), made of a flexible plastic and coated with a magnetic material, have become popular as backing store for mini and microcomputers. They are available in two sizes, standard (8 inch diameter) and mini ($5\frac{1}{4}$ inch diameter), and a number of different ways of storing the data on a surface are used, all based on tracks and sectors.

The disk is sealed inside a protective cover which has a portion removed through which the read/write head can access the disk surface (Fig. 3.16). A typical minifloppy disk can store over 100 K bytes (characters) and it may be double-sided.

WINCHESTER DISKS Although floppy disks are much more reliable than tape, and have faster access to data, they are still slow in terms of computing technology and their capacity is low. The Winchester disk system is a solution to these problems. One or more disks are held in a drive which is sealed. The disks are either $5\frac{1}{4}$ or 8 inches in diameter and they are hard, not flexible. Much greater precision is possible in reading from and writing to the disks, enabling faster access and greater capacity. Several megabytes (millions of characters) can be held on each disk. Since the drives are sealed, the disks cannot be removed and other disks cannot be inserted in their place. This means that the storage capacity, although high, is fixed.

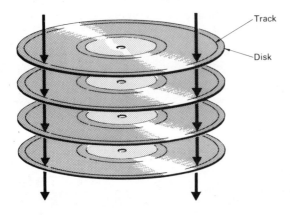

Fig 3.14   Principle of the cylinder arrangement

Fig 3.15   Floppy disk and drive for the BBC microcomputer

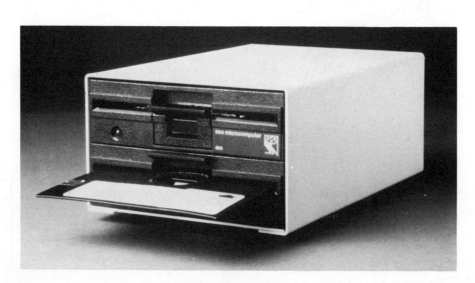

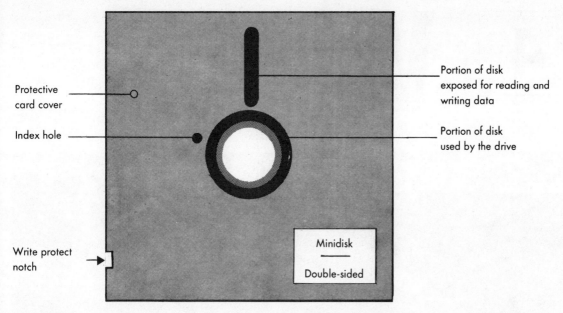

Protective
card cover

Index hole

Write protect
notch

Portion of disk
exposed for reading and
writing data

Portion of disk
used by the drive

Minidisk
—
Double-sided

Fig 3.16 Floppy disk explained

Fig 3.17 Northern Telecom's 8-inch Winchester disk drive, with the cover seal removed

4 Wages

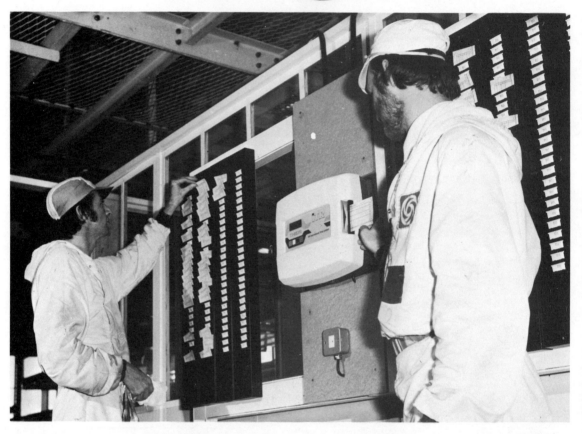

A factory which employs about 1000 people pays wages on Fridays. To calculate an employee's wage requires about 100 separate calculations. This process must be repeated for all the employees and obviously requires a lot of work – and all of the calculations must be correct. First, imagine that you had to do all of those calculations. How long would you expect it to take? Would you get them all correct? Secondly, how would you feel if you found that your wages were less than they

should be? What would you do if they were more than you had expected?

Can you suggest what data is needed to calculate a weekly wage? Some items are: hours worked, days off sick, tax code. Try to compile a list, with as many items as you can think of, including anything which would affect the wage paid.

Some people work in factories, some in offices, and some, like teachers, do not work the same number of hours every day. Try to

Fig 4.1   Wage slip

FIELDS MANUFACTURING			Date: 16/4/82		
Name: R CRANE			Works number: 15937		
Nat Ins no: ZX157634C Tax code: 215H			Week no: 2		

Earnings			Deductions		To date	
Basic					Gross pay	305.00
Hrs	40	140.00	Nat Ins	12.01	Taxable pay	214.90
O/time			Pens	3.50	Nat Ins	23.64
Hrs	3	15.00	Inc Tax	32.98	Tax	64.47
					Pens	7.00
TOTAL		155.00	TOTAL	48.49	NET PAY	106.51

think of some ways in which the data about the number of hours worked could be collected. What happens when an employee arrives at work and when the day is over? Is it the same for people who work at night? What happens if you are late for work? Some people are paid wages and others are paid salaries. Is there a difference? For what sorts of jobs are salaries paid? If necessary, your teacher will be able to help you answer some of these questions. Look at the diagram of the wage slip (Fig. 4.1). How many pieces of information does it carry?

Calculating wages

Imagine that you are to be paid for your schoolwork. The rates of pay are:

£1.00 per hour at school
£1.50 per hour for homework during the week
£2.00 per hour for homework at the weekend

You must pay 10% of your earnings to the school fund. If you are absent for up to and including 3 days, your wage will be paid at the rate of £5 per day. For absence of more than 3 days, a sick note must be provided and you can claim for sickness benefit, but no wage is paid for these days absent. Estimate your hours, to the nearest quarter of an hour, for last week, and fill in the details in the form (Fig. 4.2).

Use the information to calculate your own wage for last week.

RATE	HOURS WORKED	MONEY EARNED	
£1.00			
£1.50			
£2.00			
			◀ TOTAL
NUMBER OF DAYS SICK	RATE		
	£5		◀ SICK PAY
			◀ TOTAL
	LESS 10%		
			◀ TOTAL

Fig 4.2   Hours sheet

1 How long did it take you?
2 Have you checked the answer?
3 If a computer were going to do this calculation, what data would have to be put in for
   each person?
4 What data is common to all the calculations? Such data could be part of the
   calculating program.

The data on your form can be typed into the computer. Your teacher will run a Wages program for the whole classs; make sure that your data is correct.

Wages

You are ready now to input your data into the computer running the Wages program. The first part of the program deals with the input of data. Obviously, this can be a tedious and time-consuming task, and it is also likely that errors will be made. It is important to realise that, however quickly and accurately the computer can calculate, the results will be worthless if the data on which those calculations are based is wrong.

It helps, therefore, if the data input can be made easy and if the data can be **validated** as it is input. The screen appears as in Fig. 4.3.

Data input

The arrow indicates where the data will be entered. After typing the student number, press the SPACE bar and the arrow will move. Continue until all the data for one student is on the screen. If you have made a mistake, keep pressing the SPACE bar until the arrow is positioned correctly. Retype the data and it will overwrite the data already there. The DELETE key will delete characters one at a time.

When you are satisfied that the data is correct, press the RETURN key and the data will be accepted.

Data validation

Since a wide range of input values is possible, only simple checks are made at this stage. Only whole numbers in the range 1 to 30 are allowed for your class as student numbers. The remaining input data must consist of not more than 5 digits and not more than one decimal point, or can simply be the word STOP. Numbers are rounded to two decimal places.

Further validation occurs before the wage calculation is made.

70

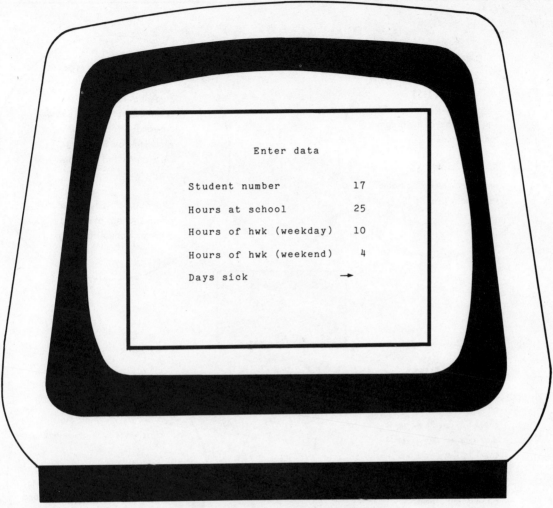

```
              Enter data


Student number            17

Hours at school           25

Hours of hwk (weekday)    10

Hours of hwk (weekend)     4

Days sick                 →
```

Fig 4.3 Screen display for Wages data input

	Maximum permitted
Hours at school	30
Hours homework (weekday)	25
Hours homework (weekend)	10
Days sick	3

Also, allowing for one school day as 6 hours, the sum total of time at school and off sick must not exceed 30 hours.

Do you think that these limits are reasonable? Can you think of any others that could be used? Why is the student number used instead of the name?

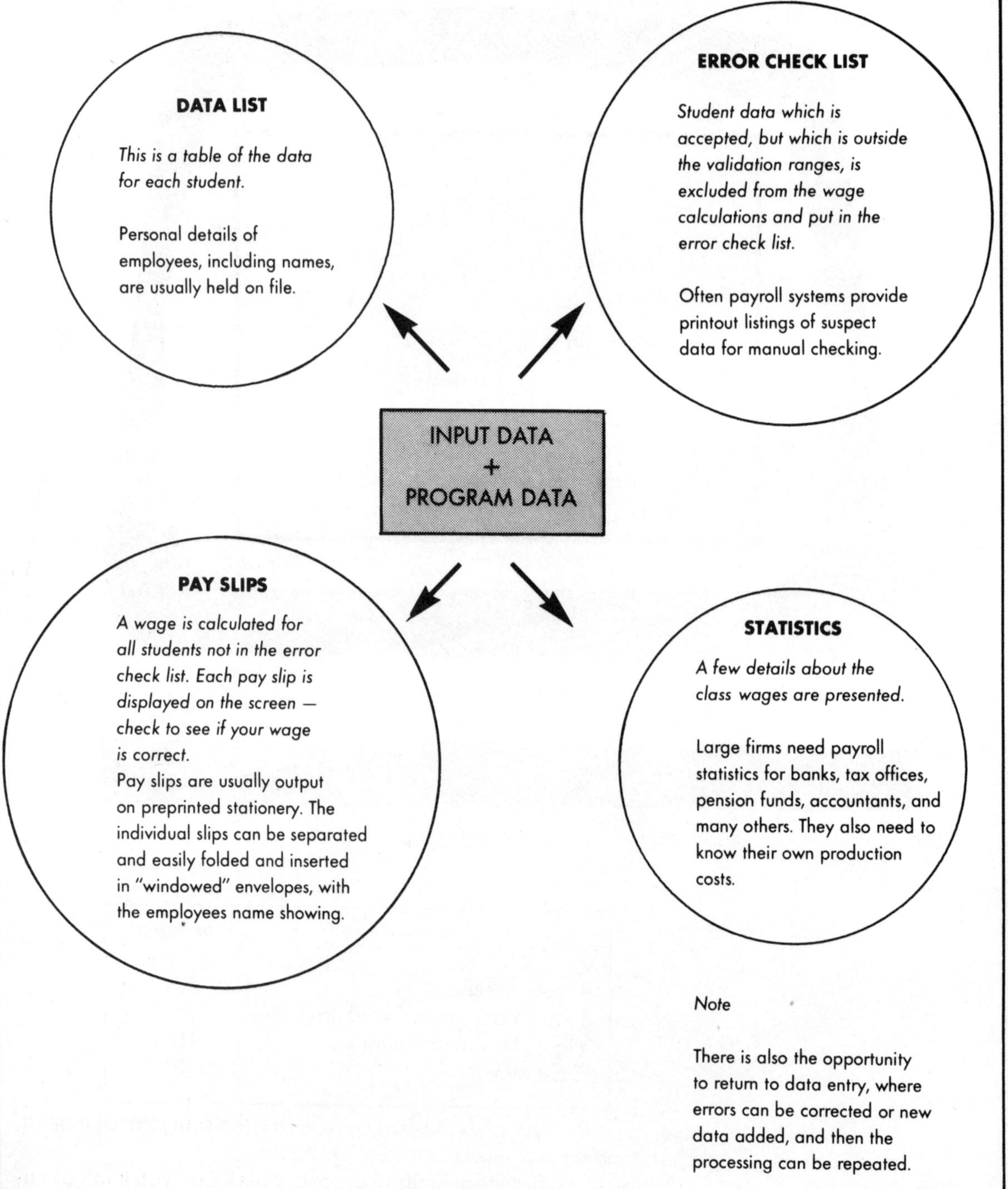

DATA LIST

This is a table of the data for each student.

Personal details of employees, including names, are usually held on file.

ERROR CHECK LIST

Student data which is accepted, but which is outside the validation ranges, is excluded from the wage calculations and put in the error check list.

Often payroll systems provide printout listings of suspect data for manual checking.

**INPUT DATA
+
PROGRAM DATA**

PAY SLIPS

A wage is calculated for all students not in the error check list. Each pay slip is displayed on the screen — check to see if your wage is correct.
Pay slips are usually output on preprinted stationery. The individual slips can be separated and easily folded and inserted in "windowed" envelopes, with the employees name showing.

STATISTICS

A few details about the class wages are presented.

Large firms need payroll statistics for banks, tax offices, pension funds, accountants, and many others. They also need to know their own production costs.

Note

There is also the opportunity to return to data entry, where errors can be corrected or new data added, and then the processing can be repeated.

Fig 4.4   Wages menu options

Information

A menu of options is provided for the selection of reports (Fig. 4.4). When you have chosen a report, simply type its number. There is no need to press RETURN.

After the program has been run, answer the following questions:
1 How long did it take to put all the data in?
2 How long did it take to calculate the wages for the whole class?
3 Was any of the input data rejected? (If so, then why?)
4 Draw up a list of the other quantities the computer calculated. Which did you think was the most useful? Can you think of anything else the computer could have done?
5 What do you think are the problems of calculating wages on a computer?
6 Does money have to be paid out? What part do the banks play in paying wages? Can you think of one benefit of not paying out actual cash?

Updating files

It has already been pointed out that, each week, when the wages are calculated, some of the data used is constant (i.e. it is the same as the previous week) and some is different (i.e. it varies from week to week). Payroll systems use files of data. There is a **master file** of detailed facts about employees, and a **transaction file** of the details of their work throughout the current week (Fig. 4.5).

Fig. 4.6 is an example of a single **record** from a master file that could be used for your class's wages calculations.

Fig 4.5 Distinction between master file and transaction file

MASTER FILE

contains
● personal data on employees, e.g. name, address.
● running totals, e.g. wage paid, tax paid so far.

TRANSACTION FILE

contains
● data for this week's wage calculation.

Fig 4.6 One record in master file

STUDENT NAME	NO.	TOTAL WAGES SO FAR	DAYS SICK
J . SMITH	1 2	3 6 . 5 0	2

The whole master file would be made up of about 30 records similar to this one. The record shown has 4 **fields**: for the name, student number, total wages paid so far, and the number of days off sick.

1 How many characters are there in each field?
2 What is the total number of characters in the record?
3 Could the data in each field take up more than the number of characters allowed? Find out the longest name in your class. What would the highest student number be? How much could you earn in a whole year? (Look at Fig. 4.2.)
4 If there was a record, like the one shown in Fig. 4.6, for every member of your class, how many characters would there be in the whole master file?

Changes have to be made to the master file when an employee joins or leaves the payroll or if the details alter.

The totals in each record of the master file are **updated** by writing in new data from the current week's transaction file.

The details of the transaction file alter from week to week. A record in the transaction file might look like Fig. 4.7.

1 How many fields are there? How many characters are there in each field? Are the fields large enough?
2 Why is the student name not included?
3 How many characters would there be in the whole class transaction file?
4 From the transaction record given, calculate the wage and update the master file record by redrawing it and writing in the new data.

STUDENT NO.	HOURS AT SCHOOL	HOURS OF HWK (WEEKDAY)	HOURS OF HWK (WEEKEND)	DAYS SICK
1 2 2 5	8	6	0	

Fig 4.7 One record in transaction file

A Factory Payroll

A certain factory in East Anglia has facilities for processing, storing and transporting frozen foods. A computer department provides management with information on production, distribution logging, engineering planning/recording, as well as running a weekly payroll.

The wages for 1200 employees at the main site, and a further 1200 at a factory in a nearby site are processed on Tuesday of each week ready to pay the employees on Thursday. Although the computer run takes only about an hour for each factory, the system for collecting and reconciling (cross-checking) data is extensive (Figs. 4.8 and 4.9).

The computer payroll program has to perform this task for all the employees, every week. Each time, a new master file is created, but the old one is not simply discarded. Usually a number of **Generations** of the files are kept for security back-up purposes, in case the master file is corrupted or destroyed accidentally. The most recent file is called the **Son**, and the earlier versions are referred to as the **Father** and **Grandfather**.

Accuracy of data

It is crucially important that the data used for computer payrolls is accurate. Often, each employee will have a company number. Since the data is found by using this number, it must be the correct one, and check digits, like those used for ISBN codes on books, are sometimes used. Checks can be built in to the wage-calculating computer program in order to validate the collected data. (Some of your class data may have been rejected during this process.)

Totals can be calculated of the number of employees, the hours worked, and the amounts paid, so that cross-checks at the end of the payroll run will reveal any errors. Employee numbers can be totalled and used as a check on the accuracy of the data. A meaningless total, like this, is referred to as a **hash total**.

Data collection

The payroll calculations are made more difficult by employees in the factory not always staying on the same job throughout a week, or even a day. Production bottlenecks, extra demand or breakdowns of machinery may make it necessary to switch some employees from one task to others, and each task may have its own hourly rate of pay. Work record sheets are completed by recorders in the factory and these sheets provide the data for the payroll run. Clock cards are also used but these are for reconciling the total hours worked.

Information

Some employees receive their pay as cash in a pay packet. Others, with bank accounts, are paid by credit transfer. Printed information sheets or computer magnetic tapes are produced to enable local bank branches to make these transfers to the appropriate employee

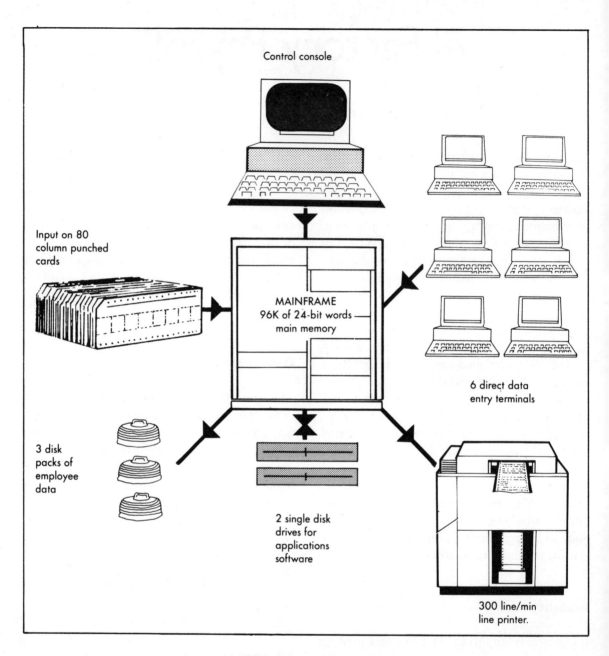

Control console

Input on 80
column punched
cards

MAINFRAME
96K of 24-bit words
main memory

6 direct data
entry terminals

3 disk
packs of
employee
data

2 single disk
drives for
applications
software

300 line/min
line printer.

Fig 4.8 System hardware

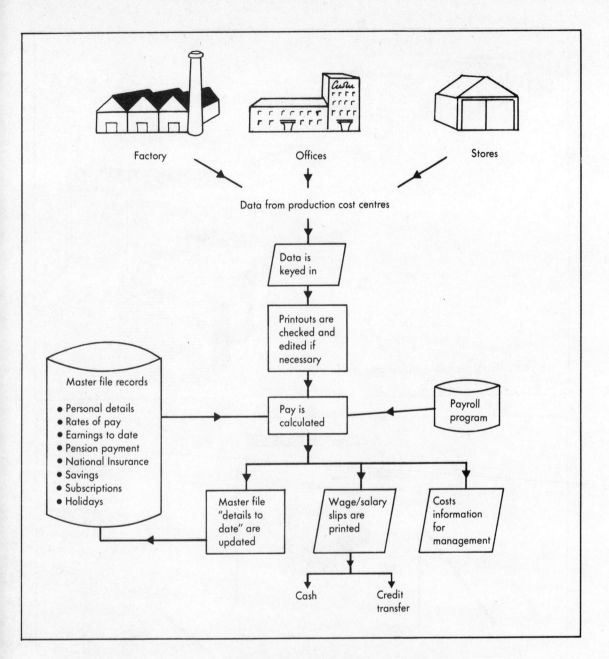

Fig 4.9 Payroll system

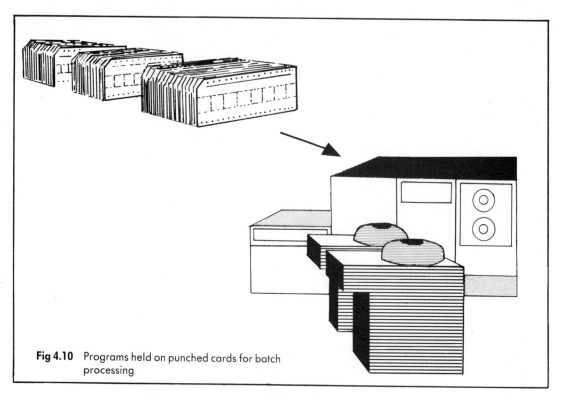

Fig 4.10 Programs held on punched cards for batch processing

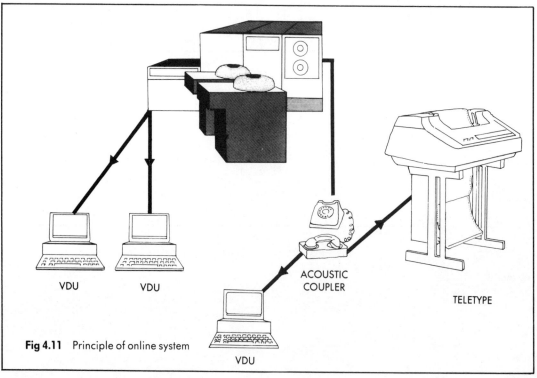

VDU   VDU

ACOUSTIC
COUPLER

TELETYPE

Fig 4.11 Principle of online system

VDU

accounts. The master file is automatically up-dated as the processing is carried out, and listings of possible errors are produced for checking by the wages department. Analysis of hours worked in the factory, as shown by the various product centres, provides information that is vital to management. They need to know quickly and accurately the costs of pro-duction in the factory.

Security of data

Many of the files are large and increasing in size. The data held has to be protected. Back-up copies are kept safe in other buildings, and a number of generations (grandfather, father and son) of updated files are stored so that the information could be compiled again if a disas-ter occurred. In the event of a breakdown, other computer installations in the area, with similar hardware, can offer computer time to run the payroll. Although the payroll is only one of a number of computer services pro-vided, it is vital that it is run on time so that the employees receive their pay on time, every week.

Batch and online processing

It may be convenient to wait until all data has been collected before computer processing begins. If this is not possible, then the proces-sing may be done when enough data has been collected, and then repeated as necessary when more data is available – this is called **batch processing** (Fig. 4.10). It can refer to batches of programs being run, one after the other, as well as to batches of data. The jobs wait in a queue and are then processed in sequence.

Batch processing is useful in situations where the collection of data might be slow, and the computer would have to wait, idle, before more data arrives. Also, if communica-tion links are difficult, batch processing might be preferable.

An alternative to batch processing is to have a direct link to the computer processor, whilst a program is running. This is referred to as being **online**. Data can be asked for and acted on immediately, or stored for later processing. The direct link can be provided by a telephone line, in which case a device called a modem or acoustic coupler is required to convert the sound signals to electronic pulses. (See Fig. 4.11.)

Where a number of users are connected directly to a computer, the computer must offer processing time to each one. This is referred to as **time-sharing**. The organisation of time-sharing requires an operating system to decide priorities and to monitor each user's demands. The aim is to provide a service for each user such that each thinks they are the only user, unaware of other users. Batch pro-cessing can be carried out in a multiprogram-ming system, and this helps the computer to make the most efficient use of its slower peripheral equipment.

5 Words

The electronic office

As offices have begun to use the more sophisticated equipment which electronics has made possible, so a new phrase "the electronic office" has been used to describe the modern office.

Traditionally, offices have been the place where letters and reports are produced, where information is stored and retrieved, and where information is despatched to, or received from, other offices, usually by post or telephone. All these tasks are vital to any commercial enterprise.

The introduction of electronics to the processing of data, in order to produce information, has led to the development of **information technology**. This will have an impact in three broad areas of office activity.

INFORMATION STORAGE AND RETRIEVAL USING COMPUTERS

This enables large amounts of data to be stored, easily cross-referenced and quickly accessed.

TRANSMISSION OF DATA BETWEEN OFFICES

Offices can use computers linked by the existing telephone network, television signals, or even worldwide satellite communications.

WORD PROCESSING

Printed documents can be created, edited and stored electronically or magnetically. High-quality output can be produced.

A **word processor** is designed to aid the preparation of text. Pages of text can be created and corrected very easily, and once created they can be stored for future use and modified at any time.

Sometimes the word processor is purchased as a complete system, dedicated to this single job. It will comprise a microprocessor, disk drives, VDU, keyboard, printer, and software (Fig. 5.1). Alternatively, a word processing package can be purchased to run on an existing computer system.

Word processing

PREPARING TEXT A page of text is produced by "typing" onto a visual display screen, using a conventional QWERTY keyboard. The words appear at the top of the screen and remain in view as additional lines are typed. Scrolling occurs only when the bottom of the screen has been reached. As the next line of text appears on the bottom of the screen, the whole screen display moves up one line, and the top line disappears off the top of the screen.

Margins can be set in the normal way and carriage return occurs automatically once the right-hand margin has been set. A word which overlaps this margin will automatically be thrown onto the next line. This means that an operator can give his or her full attention to the task of typing, regardless of whether a word will fit into the remaining space on the line.

Each screenful of text is equivalent to approximately half a page of A4 typing.

SAVING TEXT A page of text, having been set up, can be stored on a floppy disk until it is required for printing, correcting or updating. The equivalent of 50 full pages of A4 text can be stored on one $5\frac{1}{4}$ inch floppy disk.

EDITING TEXT Very often, the document which comes back from a typing pool is not the final version that is required. The typist or the document originator may have made mistakes. Circumstances may have changed since the document was first drafted, or the originator may have changed his or her mind: extra information must be included; something must be removed; a section must be reworded to improve the style; the order of paragraphs must be changed; the presentation must be altered.

When this happens under a conventional typing arrangement, there is only one thing to do. Begin again. This takes time, and time is money. With a word processor there is no need to begin again. Corrections can be made to text which has been saved on disk. Single characters, words and lines of text can be deleted or inserted; paragraphs deleted, moved, broken or merged (joined together); and text justified. Clearly, the longer a document is and the more complicated its presentation, the more useful the word processor becomes.

The Screen Unit: 15-inch display screen; 24 lines, each of 80 characters; 384 different characters; gold characters on dark bronze background; facilities include vertical and horizontal ruling, scrolling, bolding, underlining, diagrams, tables, multiple columns.

The Keyboard: a standard typewriter keyboard, plus a group of function and control keys which permit automatic editing, formatting, screen positioning, file indexing, global searching, merging, etc.

The Control Unit: twin floppy disk drive with maximum capacity for each disk of 100 pages of A4 text. The word processing program is held in the 16-bit microprocessor of the unit, leaving the disks free for data storage.

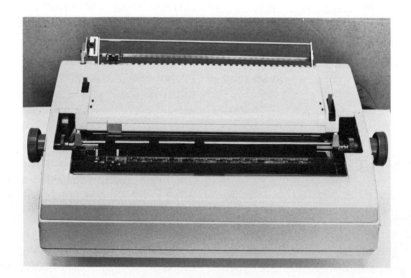

The Printer: a high-quality daisy wheel printer, operating at 60 characters per sec (700 words per sec). A range of 124-character daisy wheels, and automatic sheet feed or tractor feed, can be used.

Fig 5.1a Components of a word processor system: the ICL DRS system

Fig 5.1*b* An ICL Desk Top System with 100-key keyboard dedicated to data processing, data entry and word processing

Fig 5.1*c* An IBM Office System with word and information processing facilities. Such a system can link with telephone networks for text distribution

JUSTIFYING TEXT AND ALTERING THE COLUMN WIDTH A facility which most word processors provide is text justification. Look carefully at Fig. 5.2. The text on the left is unjustified. By the touch of a key, it can be converted to justified text in a matter of seconds.

As well as justifying text, the word processor can alter the width of a column with equally impressive ease and speed. Fig. 5.2 was converted to Fig. 5.3 in this way.

The text in books, newspapers and magazines normally appears in neat columns, the last letter of one line appearing beneath the last letter of the previous line. This is referred to as justified text. Using a normal typewriter this is a difficult and time consuming effect to achieve. However, it greatly enhances presentation and may be particularly desirable in some cases, perhaps in the presentation of reports which are to be published. A word processor can justify a complete page of text within seconds. The passage on the right was produced in this way.

The text in books, newspapers and magazines normally appears in neat columns, the last letter of one line appearing beneath the last letter of the previous line. This is referred to as justified text. Using a normal typewriter this is a difficult and time consuming effect to achieve. However, it greatly enhances presentation and may be particularly desirable in some cases, perhaps in the presentation of reports which are to be published. A word processor can justify a complete page of text within seconds.

Fig 5.2   Unjustified and justified text

The text in books, newspapers and magazines normally appears in neat columns, the last letter of one line appearing beneath the last letter of the previous line. This is referred to as justified text. Using a normal typewriter this is a difficult and time consuming effect to achieve. However, it greatly enhances presentation and may be particularly desirable in some cases, perhaps in the presentation of reports which are to be published. A word processor can justify a complete page of text within seconds.

Fig 5.3   Justified wide-column text

Keyboards

Since 1873 when the first commercial type-writers were introduced, keyboards have been used to provide clear printed documents in offices. Keyboards are also used as input devices for computers. They are widely used at present, but this may not continue to be so in the future. Can you think of any other ways in which you would like to communicate with a computer? What other methods of input to a computer have you come across in this book?

Typewriters which have a standard key layout for the letters of the alphabet are said to have a QWERTY keyboard. Where do you think this name comes from? Copy the grid (Fig. 5.4) and fill in only the letters and numbers as they are found on a standard keyboard.

You will have noticed that the letters are not in alphabetical order. See if you can find out why this layout was chosen.

Examine carefully the other keys around the letters and numbers. Some of them are used for special purposes. Find out what they are used for. Typing usually produces UPPER CASE and lower case letters. How are these produced on the Keyboard? What do you press for a space? On a display screen (and on some typewriters) it is possible to delete characters. Which key is used to delete?

Fig 5.4 Keyboard layout

Words

Your teacher can provide you with a program that will enable you to use some of the facilities of word processors. Remember, this program only *simulates* the functions of a word processor. The real thing is usually more flexible and much faster in operation.

By using the command C, a full list of the commands can be produced on the screen at any time whilst the program is running, and without losing the text. A full list is:

I	insert
D	delete
W	width
M	move
E	exchange
T	type
P	print
S	save
L	load
C	commands
Q	quit
R	restart

A detailed description of these commands is given on pages 91 to 93. The area for text on your screen allows 16 lines of 36 characters. The lines are numbered down the left-hand edge. To specify the line where editing is to take place, follow the command letter with the line number. For example

T 12   type characters on line 12

If you omit the line number, then line 1 will be assumed.

When the program is running, you will see that there are two areas on the screen. The large area at the top of the screen will display the text that you type, with the lines numbered from 1 to 16 down the left-hand edge to help you to identify them. Before you can enter text, you must use one of the commands. The chosen command appears in the lines at the bottom of the screen (Fig. 5.5).

You can discover some of the features of this word processing program by experimenting with the commands.

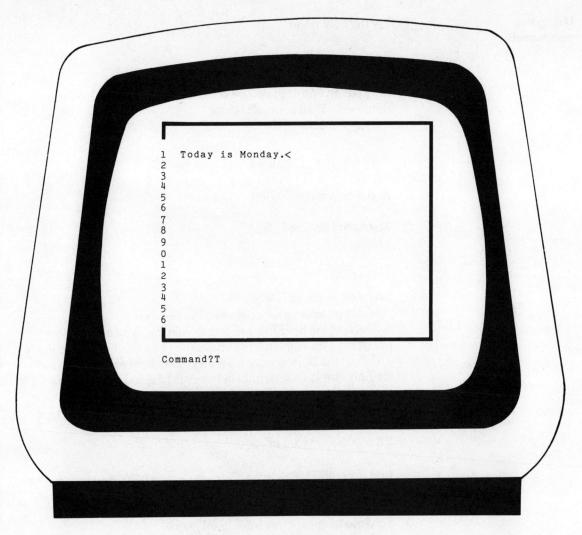

```
 1    Today is Monday.<
 2
 3
 4
 5
 6
 7
 8
 9
 0
 1
 2
 3
 4
 5
 6

Command?T
```

Fig 5.5 Screen display for starting Words

Using the commands

1 Try the command

`T`

to **type** on line 1. (If you omit the line number, line 1 will be assumed.) Then press RETURN.
   Type the sentence:

`Today is Monday`

and then press RETURN.

2 To **insert** on line 1, type

`I`

and then press RETURN.
   Insertion takes place between the pointers ⟩⟨.
   Pressing the SHIFT key together with the ⟩ key moves both pointers to the right, and pressing the ⟨ key moves them to the left.
   (When the pointers are on the extreme left of the screen, only the ⟨ pointer is visible, until the ⟩ key is pressed. Both pointers will then become visible.)
   Move the pointers to the space after the word "is" and type

`the day after`

and press RETURN. Is the spacing correct? The pointers must be positioned very carefully.

3 To **delete** characters from line 1, type

`D`

and press RETURN. Move the pointers to the start of the word "after". Pressing the space bar opens the pointers. Repeat this until "after" is surrounded by the pointers, and then press RETURN.

4 **Moving** text from one part of the screen to another is very similar. Type

`M`

and press RETURN. Proceed as before to surround "Monday", and then press RETURN. You will then be asked which line you would like to move the word to. Choose a line, line 3, for example. Type

3

and press RETURN. Move the pointers along line 3 to the place where you would like the word to appear, and then press RETURN again.

5   You can **exchange** "Monday" for "Tuesday" by typing

E/Monday/Tuesday/

and pressing RETURN.

6   Finally, **alter the width** of the lines of text on the screen by typing

W10

followed by RETURN. The lines will change to 10 characters long and will be centred on the screen.

When you decrease the line length, there will, automatically, be fewer characters on the screen display. Any characters from the bottom of the screen that are lost in this way will not be returned. Also, any characters that are lost from the right-hand end of a line, through inserting or exchanging, will not be returned.

There are also commands for loading, saving and printing text. These are explained on pages 92 and 93.

You are now ready to try an exercise. Type

R

and press RETURN to clear the screen of text, to enable you to start afresh.

Redcar

The following piece of text can be typed in or, if you wish, loaded from tape or disk using the L command. The text should be set up as shown in Fig. 5.6.

1 Exchange, using the E instruction, the colour "red" for the colour "blue". Has this change worked successfully?

2 Complete the change of colour from red to blue, in the text, using the other commands available. Quite clearly there is more than one way of doing this. Before you start, think carefully about which commands you are going to use.

Make sure that no letters are lost at the ends of lines, that all "red" has changed to "blue", and that any unwanted changes are put back to the way they should be.

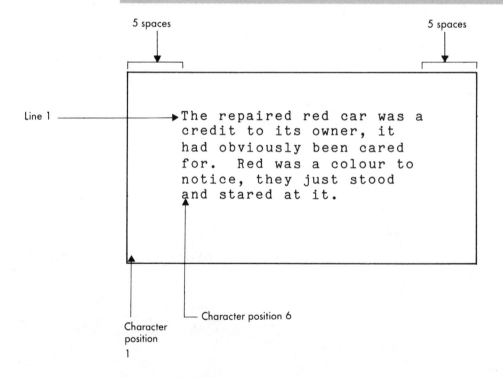

Fig 5.6 Text arrangement for Redcar

Commands

FUNCTION   Insert
COMMAND   `I n`   where n is the line number 1–16.
DESCRIPTION The pointers are moved across the line by the
`)(` keys. Characters are inserted between the pointers
until the RETURN key is pressed. The DELETE key can
be used to rub out the previous character inserted. If
n is omitted, then line 1 is assumed.

EXAMPLES   `I  ,    I 12`

FUNCTION   Delete
COMMAND   `D n`   where n is the line number 1–16.
DESCRIPTION The pointers are moved across the line by the `)(` keys.
The pointers are opened by pressing the SPACE bar.
Characters surrounded by the pointers are deleted
on pressing the RETURN key. If n is omitted, then line
1 is assumed.

EXAMPLES   `D  ,    D 13`

FUNCTION   Alter line width
COMMAND   `W n`   where n is the line width 1–36.
DESCRIPTION The width of each line is changed to the size given in
the command. The lines are centred on the page.
Characters lost from the bottom of the page, during
the change of line width, cannot be recovered.
Initially the line width is 36 characters. The message

`Please wait for the command prompt...`

is issued while the new page format appears.

EXAMPLES   `W 10 ,   W 36`

FUNCTION   Move characters
COMMAND   `M n`   where n is the line number 1–16.
DESCRIPTION The pointers are moved across the line by the `)(` keys.
The pointers are opened by pressing the SPACE bar.
Characters surrounded by the pointers can be
moved by pressing the RETURN key. A prompt

`Move to`

is given, and the line to which the characters are to be moved should be typed in. After RETURN is pressed, the pointers can be moved to where a copy of the character string is required, on the chosen line. The characters appear in position on pressing RETURN. If n is omitted, then line 1 is assumed.

EXAMPLES   `M4`

`Move to 6`

FUNCTION   Exchange one character string for another
COMMAND

`E/character string 1/character string 2/`

DESCRIPTION   All occurrences of character string 1 are replaced by character string 2. Since the whole screen must be searched, the process is rather slow, and a warning

`Please wait for the command prompt...`

message is given.

EXAMPLES   `E/RIGHT/WRONG/`   `E/T//`   `E/S/SS/`

FUNCTION   Type characters to the screen
COMMAND   `Tn`   where n is the line number 1–16.
DESCRIPTION   The pointers are moved across the line by the ⟩⟨ keys. Characters typed appear between the pointers. The DELETE key can be used to rub out the previous typed character. If n is omitted, then line 1 is assumed.

EXAMPLE   `T12`

FUNCTION   Print
COMMAND   `P`
DESCRIPTION   The text on the screen is output to the printer. The message

`Make sure the printer is switched on.`
`Type A to abandon, or just RETURN to continue.`

appears.

FUNCTION	Save
COMMAND	S
DESCRIPTION	The text on the screen can be saved in a named file. The message

```
Make sure the correct tape/disk is ready.
Type A to abandon, or just RETURN to continue
```

appears. If the option to abandon is not taken, the prompt

```
File name?
```

is given.
The file name can contain up to 6 characters.

FUNCTION	Load
COMMAND	L
DESCRIPTION	The text in a saved file may be loaded and displayed on the screen. The message

```
Make sure the correct tape/disk is ready.
Type A to abandon, or just RETURN to continue.
```

appears. If the option to abandon is not taken, the prompt

```
File name?
```

is given.

FUNCTION	Display the commands
COMMAND	C
DESCRIPTION	A list of the commands is displayed. Pressing RETURN returns the text.

FUNCTION	Exit from the program (quit)
COMMAND	Q
DESCRIPTION	After pressing RETURN the program will terminate.

FUNCTION	Restart
COMMAND	R
DESCRIPTION	Used to clear the screen before entering new text.

Some applications of word processing

MAILSHOTS One of the tasks for which a word processor is often used is addressing. Consider the case where an organisation distributes a newsletter to each of its 5000 members once a month. Not only is manual addressing a very time-consuming and monotonous task, it is prone to human error. Using a word processor to establish a list of names and addresses can produce address labels, in quantity, as often as required, tirelessly and accurately.

PERSONALISED DOCUMENTS In the prepared newsletter, a space can be left for the recipient's name. The word processor reads a name from the address file and inserts it in the space which has been flagged.

A more sophisticated way of personalising documents is to prepare them with "gaps", which are filled in when the document is sent out (Fig. 5.7). Clearly, the longer and more complicated the document or letter, and the more often it has to be sent out, the more useful the word processor becomes.

```
(Date)                                      Dud Electrical Goods
                                            62 Cowboy Plain
                                            LEEDS
                                            LS1 4PR

(Addressee)                                 Tel:  0532  91919


Dear  (Name)

Thank you for your order, invoice number  (Figure).

We regret to inform you that the items listed below are temporarily
out of stock.  There will be a  (Figure)  day delay in fulfilling
your requirements.

Item numbers:
(Numbers)

Yours sincerely




T Jones
Sales Manager
```

Fig 5.7 Personalised document with gaps

ACCOUNTS Word processors often have an arithmetic facility, which is particularly useful for preparing accounts and reports which contain arithmetic of a basic kind. The facility includes addition, subtraction, multiplication, division, and the calculation of percentages.

First of all we set up an account shown in Fig. 5.8.

Given the correct instructions, columns will be added, differences calculated and results automatically inserted in the correct places. The final document will look like Fig. 5.9.

```
              AZTEC SUPPLIES PLC

          Year ended March 31


                1983            1982      Change    %

     ITEM

     Carried forward    16032.76        14752.81
     Purchases         710112.24       664940.79
     Wages              23479.61        21506.29
     Maintenance         1782.96         1256.13
     Insurance           1345.12         1182.45
     Rentals              703.55          672.36
     Transport          13802.42        11552.14
     Miscellaneous        491.03          462.51

     TOTAL

     Stock in hand      89217.82        82054.71

     COST TOTAL
```

Fig 5.8 First accounts document

```
              AZTEC SUPPLIES PLC

          Year ended March 31


                1983            1982      Change      %

     ITEM

     Carried forward    16032.76        14752.81    1279.95    8.68
     Purchases         710112.24       664940.79   45171.45    6.79
     Wages              23479.61        21506.29    1973.32    9.18
     Maintenance         1782.96         1256.13     526.83   41.94
     Insurance           1345.12         1182.45     162.67   13.76
     Rentals              703.55          672.36      31.19    4.64
     Transport          13802.42        11552.14    2250.28   19.48
     Miscellaneous        491.03          462.51      28.52    6.17

     TOTAL             767749.69       716325.48   51424.21    7.18

     Stock in hand      89217.82        82054.71    7163.11    8.73

     COST TOTAL        678531.87       634270.77   44261.10    6.98
```

Fig 5.9 Final accounts document

Electronic mail

In the office of the future it may turn out that the word processor is also the terminal link to a communications network. This will enable data to be transferred using the telephone and television networks, and even using satellites. The transmission of facsimile documents using computer-controlled systems will enable the electronic storage and display of information.

The development of electronic mail has two advantages: speed and the absence of paper. Public information systems such as Prestel and Teletext are being developed and computer data banks will be available too.

It may well be the case that our traditional data/information sources will give way to electronic newspapers and electronic publishing. The ability to process text is only part of a revolution being brought about by the growth of information technology.

1 If electronic word processing equipment were available, an office manager might prepare his or her own letters. What would be the advantages and disadvantages of this?

2 See if you can find out how a newspaper is printed. Journalists who write stories are not usually concerned with how the paper is printed or how the pages are laid out. Who does these jobs? Could a word processor be used? What problems do you think the introduction of electronic printing equipment would create?

3 Two public information systems are now available. Teletext (CEEFAX and ORACLE) uses the television networks and PRESTEL uses the telephone network. What are the differences between these systems? Can anybody use them?

Printers

Word processor systems, like most micro-computers, output their hard copy on printers which print a single character at a time. There are two popular techniques in use: the dot matrix printer and the daisy wheel printer. Mainframe computers use line printers.

DOT MATRIX PRINTERS Matrix printers, priced at a few hundred pounds, tend to be the cheaper of the two types. They produce their characters in a matrix of dots, as shown in Fig. 5.10.

The dots are produced by a single vertical line of needles, which make impact with an inked ribbon. There are a number of different dot patterns in use, such as 7×5, 9×7, 9×9, and printing can be bi-directional, giving speeds of about 100 characters per second.

DAISY WHEEL PRINTERS Most daisy wheel printers are at least twice as expensive as dot matrix printers. They use, as the name suggests, a wheel with the character-set engraved at the ends of spokes (Fig. 5.11), and impact is made with an inked ribbon. The wheel is about 3 inches (76 mm) in diameter, and different wheels for different type styles can easily be fitted. The quality of printing is generally higher than that from dot matrix printers, and is good enough for office correspondence. The printing can also be bi-directional but the speed is about half that of dot matrix printers.

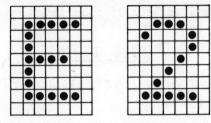

Fig 5.10 Formation of Characters in a 9 × 7 matrix of dots

Fig 5.11 Daisy wheel

GB Roman PS

Work can be presented in a variety of type faces by simply changing the daisy wheel.

TILE ITALIC

Work can be presented in a variety of type faces by simply changing the daisy wheel

GB Titan 10

Work can be presented in a variety of type faces by simply changing the daisy wheel.

GB Trend PS

Work can be presented in a variety of type faces by simply changing the daisy wheel.

CUBIC PS

Work can be presented in a variety of type faces by simply changing the daisy wheel

MADELEINE P.S

Work can be presented in a variety of type faces by simply changing the daisy wheel

GB Elite 12

Work can be presented in a variety of type faces by simply changing the daisy wheel.

Fig 5.12 Various type styles available on a daisy wheel printer

LINE PRINTERS Mainframe computers, by comparison, usually output on line printers, which print a complete line of perhaps 120 characters at a time. Barrel (or drum) printers (Fig. 5.13) have the character-set embossed around the barrel at each character position. As the barrel rotates once, hammers strike at the precise moment to print the correct character at every position along the line in which it is required – all of the As, then all the Bs, all the Cs, etc.

Other methods are to move the characters on a chain (Fig. 5.14) or on a sliding bar.

Line printers are used for large volumes of output and they can print at 1000 lines per minute. How many characters per second is this equivalent to?

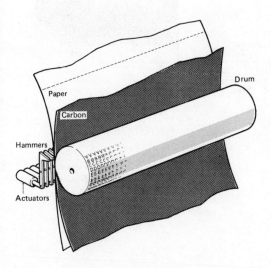

Fig 5.13 Barrel (or drum) printer

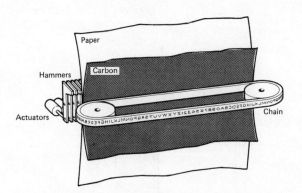

Fig 5.14 Chain printer

Growth of information technology

Information technology includes the communications networks for the transmission of data, as well as the computing hardware and services for its processing. Worldwide business for I.T. is increasing rapidly. Some statistics for 1980 are shown in Figs. 5.15 and 5.16.

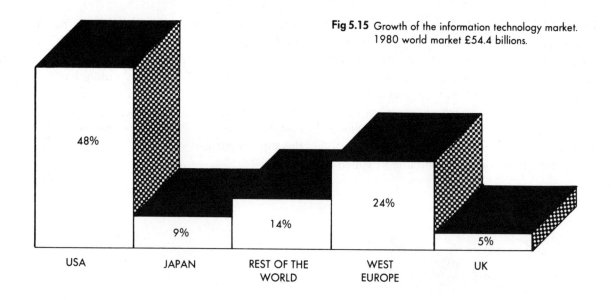

Fig 5.15 Growth of the information technology market. 1980 world market £54.4 billions.

USA — 48%
JAPAN — 9%
REST OF THE WORLD — 14%
WEST EUROPE — 24%
UK — 5%

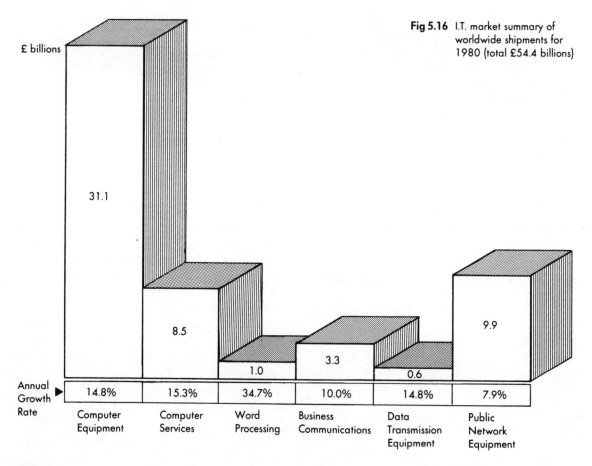

Fig 5.16 I.T. market summary of worldwide shipments for 1980 (total £54.4 billions)

£ billions

	Computer Equipment	Computer Services	Word Processing	Business Communications	Data Transmission Equipment	Public Network Equipment
£ billions	31.1	8.5	1.0	3.3	0.6	9.9
Annual Growth Rate	14.8%	15.3%	34.7%	10.0%	14.8%	7.9%

6 LAW ENFORCEMENT

Crime Story

DATE: 12 MARCH 1984

"Well, James Tovey, let's take it from the beginning," said the police officer, looking up from her notes.

"I was making a special delivery. Had to be dropped over at New City Hospital before 5 o'clock, they said."

"What were you carrying?"

"Drugs of some kind. That's our business. I work for Duprene Pharmaceuticals. Anyway, I was just approaching the City Road from Castle Avenue when I'm flagged down by this traffic cop, or at least what I thought was a traffic cop."

"What made you think that?"

"Well, he was wearin' the uniform, wasn't he? And there were these plastic bollards and a halt sign in the road."

"Is Castle Avenue busy?" she asked.

"Not usually," he replied. "Not today, anyway."

"What did you do when he flagged you down?"

"I pulled up alongside him and rolled down the window. I said, "What's up, mate? And he says, 'This is,' and pushes a gun up into me face and tells me to get out."

"And you did?"

"Too right, I did. He'd have used it."

"Why so certain?"

"Could see it in his eyes. Mad. Mad as a hatter."

"What colour?"

"Pardon?"

"His eyes. What colour were his eyes?"

A momentary pause as the gunman's eyes loomed up in his mind once again, staring out of a ghostly white face. Threatening.

"Brown!" Yes, brown," he blurted out.

"Thank you." The policewoman made a note on her pad. "Do you know anything about guns?"

"No, nothing," he said.

"So you couldn't say what type it was, or even if it was real?"

"No. Sorry." Tovey fidgeted in his seat.

"But you can say in which hand he carried it."

A grin creased the man's face. "Left. It was definitely his left. I know because he was in an awkward position when he opened the cab door. Had to cross his arms. Thought I might have a go at him," he concluded, looking across at the second police officer to gauge her reaction.

"Really?" His questioner gave him a cold appraising stare.

"Well, maybe not," he said looking down at the floor and shuffling his feet uncomfortably.

"But, you know," he said hopefully. "Actually, he was pretty big."

"How big?" Finely sharpened pencil poised.

"Taller than me, and I'm five eleven in me socks."

"Heavy?"

"Fourteen stone," he grinned. "But I'd say *he* was fourteen and a half." The policewomen showed no sign of being amused.

"How old would you say he was?"

"Thirtyish. Maybe a bit older."

"Hair?"

"Black."

"Did he have an accomplice?"

"Yeh, but I didn't see him. The one with the gun took the keys out of the ignition and threw them to this other guy who'd come up behind me. He said, 'Here, Croak, catch.'"

"Then what happened?"

"They took the box from inside and then locked me in the van. And there I had to stay until your lot turned up and let me out."

The police officer sat and looked at him for a full half minute, making him feel even more uncomfortable than before. Eventually, she said, "How does it feel to be a prime suspect?"

"You what?" he exclaimed. "I don't know nothin' about this. Only what I've told you. I've never been in trouble with the law. Check it."

"Don't worry, we will," she said, getting up and moving towards the door. "Someone on the inside is involved. Otherwise, how did they know what to look for, where and when?" With that she left the room, leaving him under the watchful gaze of the remaining police-woman.

Duprene Pharmaceuticals Employees

a   Arthur Hammond. Age 34.
    127 Saxon St., Huntston, Zone 2.
    Senior Clerk.

b   James Tovey. Age 30.
    14 Bryth Rd., Camco, Zone 8.
    Driver.

c   Joseph Jackson. Age 23.
    40 Orchard Way, Hurley, Zone 3.
    Junior Clerk.

d   Simon Jinx. Age 43.
    21 Manor Close, Crawford, Zone 2.
    Transport Manager.

e   Carol Davidson. Age 19.
    19 Hill Crest Rd., Hurley, Zone 3.
    Secretary.

a

b

c

d

e

Criminal records index

The Newland Law Enforcement Agency has a computer file on criminals convicted within the region in which the robbery occurred. After interviewing James Tovey, the police have enough information to run searches against this file in order to produce a list of suspects.

Imagine that you are an officer serving in the NLEA computer section. It is your task to run the necessary searches and so produce some leads for officers working on the case.

You are looking for three suspects:

a   The gunman
b   The man called Croak
c   A Duprene employee
    Do any Duprene employees have criminal records? If so, is there anything in their records to link them with either of the other suspects?

Deduction

When you think you have three suspects, input the command DEDUCTION in response to an input prompt. You will be invited to input the RECORD NUMBERS of each of the suspects, so keep a note of these as your search proceeds.

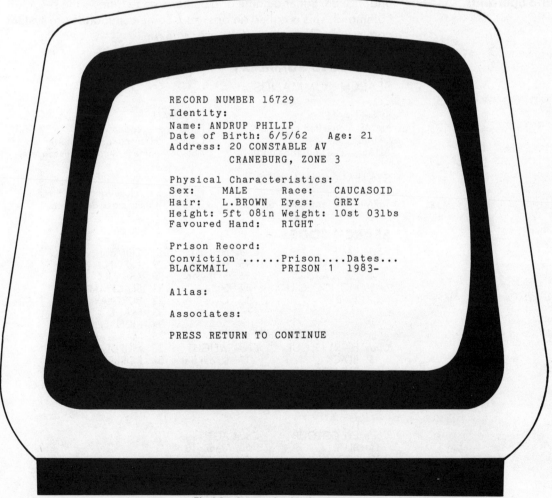

```
RECORD NUMBER 16729
Identity:
Name: ANDRUP PHILIP
Date of Birth: 6/5/62    Age: 21
Address: 20 CONSTABLE AV
         CRANEBURG, ZONE 3

Physical Characteristics:
Sex:   MALE       Race:    CAUCASOID
Hair:  L.BROWN    Eyes:    GREY
Height: 5ft 08in Weight: 10st 03lbs
Favoured Hand:    RIGHT

Prison Record:
Conviction ......Prison....Dates...
BLACKMAIL        PRISON 1  1983-

Alias:

Associates:

PRESS RETURN TO CONTINUE
```

Fig 6.1   Screen display for Crime

CR/ME

CRIME is an information retrieval program. The records are criminal records. Each record has five fields: Identity, Physical Characteristics, Criminal Record, Alias, Criminal Associates – as shown in Fig. 6.1. The records can be retrieved by a search on any of these fields.

Commands and operands

A command language is used to specify the type of search to be undertaken. Either a name or a numeric code follows the search command. This is called an *operand*. Some commands are system commands. These control the program run.

COMMAND SUMMARY

SEARCH COMMANDS

SEX=FEMALE
NAME=name (left-hand part)
CRIME=code
ALIAS=name (left-hand part)

SEX=MALE
PHYS=code/code/code/
CRIME+PHYS=code/code/code/
ASSOC=name (any consecutive letters)

SYSTEM COMMANDS

TERMINATE terminates run

CLOSE   closes access to files
DEDUCTION to make deduction

SEARCH CODES

Code	RACE	Code	HEIGHT	Code	CRIME
3	AFRICAN	15	Under 5'	29	ARSON
4	CAUCASOID	16	5' 1"–5' 6"	30	ASSAULT
5	MONGOLOID	17	5' 7"–6'	31	BLACKMAIL
		18	Over 6'	32	BURGLARY
				33	FRAUD
				34	KIDNAPPING
				35	MANSLAUGHTER
Code	HAIR COLOUR	Code	WEIGHT	36	MURDER
6	BLACK	19	Under 8 st	37	ROBBERY – ARMED
7	BLONDE	20	8 st–10 st	38	ROBBERY – BANK
8	DARK BROWN	21	10 st–14 st	39	ROBBERY – MUGGING
9	LIGHT BROWN	22	Over 14 st	40	SHOPLIFTING
10	RED				
Code	EYE COLOUR	Code	AGE		
11	BLUE	23	Under 18		
12	BROWN	24	18–20		
13	GREEN	25	21–30		
14	GREY	26	31–40		
		27	41–50		
		28	Over 50		

Passwords

When you run the program you will be invited to enter a password. No searching can take place until a valid password has been input. There are six valid passwords:

```
123
456
789
ABC
DEF
GHI
```

All have three characters. You will not see them on the screen as they are entered. Once a valid password has been input, the following user prompt appears:

```
NEW SEARCH
INPUT COMMAND
```

The use of the commands

CLOSE   The command CLOSE will close access to the system. No further searches will be allowed until another valid password is input.
Input the command CLOSE and then re-enter using another password.

NAME=   This command causes the computer to search through the records for any record with a name in the identity field which begins with the letters specified. This is called *right-hand term truncation*.
Do this search:

```
NAME=BAKER WILLIAM
```

What crime was committed by the person with this name?
Do this search:

```
NAME=WAY
```

What are the full names of any criminals whose names begin with these letters?

SPACES   No spaces should be inserted between a command and an operand (i.e. a name or numerical code).

PHYS= It is possible to search for records containing a number of related physical characteristics. For example:

white AND with red hair AND under 5' AND over 14 stone

Codes must be used in a PHYS= search. The above search will look like this:

```
PHYS=4/10/15/22/
```

Codes must be separated by /, and / must follow the last code. There must be no spaces in the search statement.

Is there a criminal record for anyone answering the above description? What is/are the record number(s).

CRIME= Again, a code is used as the operand. Only one code is permitted.

Do this search:

```
CRIME=30
```

For which crime is 30 a code? How many criminal records does this search reveal?

CRIME+PHYS= It may be useful to search for people with a criminal record who fit a particular physical description AND who have committed a particular crime.

A man answering the following description was seen running from the scene of a fire: blonde, fairly tall, quite heavy, probably in his early thirties. Is there a record for anyone answering this description who has a record for arson?

Do this search:

```
CRIME+PHYS=29/7/17/21/26/
```

What is/are their name(s) and record number(s).

ALIAS= Criminals sometimes use or are known by more than one name. This command permits a search for anyone using an alias which begins with a specified combination of letters. For example:

```
ALIAS=SMART JOHN
```

and

```
ALIAS=SMAR
```

will both locate records with the name SMART JOHN in the Alias field.

Try these searches. What is the man's real name?

ASSOC= It may be useful to establish links between known criminals during an inquiry. The command ASSOC= enables you to search the Associate field. It allows both left and right-hand term truncation. For example:

```
ASSOC=JUBB ARTHUR
ASSOC=JUBB A
ASSOC=UBB ARTHUR
ASSOC=UBB
```

will all retrieve records with the name JUBB ARTHUR in the Associate field.

Try these searches. Who is/are Arthur Jubb's associate(s)?

SEX= There are two files (collections of records): one for men, the other for women. A searcher can specify the file to be searched. For example:

```
NEW SEARCH        NEW SEARCH
INPUT COMMAND     INPUT COMMAND
?SEX=FEMALE       ?SEX=MALE
```

If the SEX= command is not used, the system defaults to a search of the Male file.

Do this search (remember to open the Female file):

```
NAME=EGGET JULIA
```

What crime did this lady commit?

TERMINATE This is the only way to exit from the program.

Both the memory in the central processor unit, and the tapes and disks used as backing store, have a finite capacity – they can store only so much data, and no more. It is important to use both economically. For this reason, data is often *coded*. This is the case with the program CRIME.

An Uncoded Record

```
UXWORTH BRIAN,3/1/48,13 KEMPS LOKE,TUFFIELD,ZONE 6,6'3", 15st
12lbs, MALE,CAUCASOID,BLACK HAIR,GREEN EYES,ARMED ROBBERY,
PRISON 2,1968-82,,,LEFT HANDED,14620
```

A Coded Record

```
UXWORTH BRIAN,3,1,48,13 KEMPS LOKE,TUFFIELD,6,6,03,15,
12,2,4,6,13,37,42,68-82,,,L,14620
```

There are 137 characters in the uncoded record and only 66 characters in the coded version, a saving of more than 50%. Codes for age, height and weight do not appear in the record at all. These are generated by the computer from the actual age, height and weight while the program is running.

Prepare an uncoded record and a coded record for yourself. There are four prison codes for men: 41, 42, 43 and 44. There is one prison code for women: 45. The last number in the record is a five-digit criminal record number.

How many characters have you saved by coding?

The Police National Computer

The Police National Computer is situated at Hendon in North London. It has the capacity to store in the region of 40 million records. These can be accessed on line from 800 terminals in police stations throughout the country. Information which previously took days to obtain can be retrieved in a matter of seconds.

1 VEHICLE OWNERS INDEX

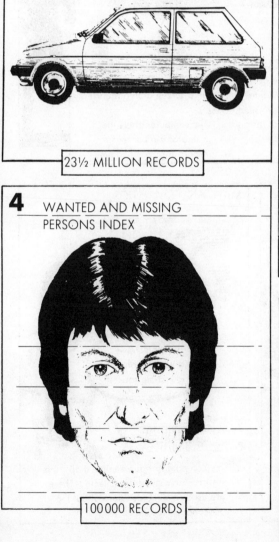

23½ MILLION RECORDS

2 DISQUALIFIED DRIVERS INDEX

170 000 RECORDS

3 STOLEN AND SUSPECT VEHICLES INDEX

100 000 RECORDS

4 WANTED AND MISSING PERSONS INDEX

100 000 RECORDS

5 FINGERPRINTS INDEX

2½ MILLION RECORDS

6 CRIMINAL RECORDS INDEX

4 MILLION RECORDS

FIGHTING CRIME

OPERATIONAL DETECTIVE WORK

Computers are fast and good at cross-referencing

Some investigations generate vast quantities of information

The infamous 'Yorkshire Ripper' case highlighted the need to use a computer. During the investigation some 30 000 names were collected.

CONTROL AND COMMAND SYSTEMS

The computer directs a patrol car to an incident. In deciding which car to send, it takes into account distance from the scene and each car's status.

Each car's position is plotted on a screen at headquarters.

The computer alerts the operator if a car fails to report at a specified time.

PAWNSHOP REPORTS

An unusual application has been developed in the city of Longbeach, California.

Pawnshop owners submit data to the police on each item pawned, and on the person who pawned it.

This data is matched with data on recorded thefts. The computer flags anyone who pawns more than 4 articles in a 30-day period.

MAPS AND STATISTICS

The map shows areas of high and low crime rate.

The computer produces crime maps and statistics from the data collected. These are used to make decisions about the allocation of resources.

Privacy

Two of the key qualities of computer systems are their capacity to store large quantities of data and to process it at very high speeds. It is not surprising that they are used to store and access information about the general public. Tax records, social security records, medical records, criminal records, driving licence records, credit rating records, employee records, mail ordering records, etc., are all stored in this way. In some cases, hundreds of thousands or even millions of records are involved.

Whether a computer or paper is used for storing this information about individuals, the basic issue of privacy is the same. People have certain expectations regarding their privacy. There are certain facts about themselves that they do not wish to be widely known. Many people, for example, are sensitive about disclosing their income – which in itself is not necessarily damaging information. It is the case with computers, however, that data can often be accessed from remote terminals via a telephone line. This ease of access is a cause for concern.

There are four principal expectations regarding personal information and privacy:

1 *Any information collected and stored should be adequate for the purpose for which it was created and not in excess of that.*

   While most people would accept the storing of personal details for an employee wages record, they might well question the inclusion of such details as: divorcee, unmarried mother, or member of CND.

2 *Information should be available only to legitimate users for legitimate purposes.*

   It would not be legitimate for a private investigator to obtain details of a record held by the police for a client wishing to vet a potential employee.

3 *All details held about individuals should be accurate.*

   A person might be indifferent to the fact that their birthdate was recorded as 1951 instead of 1952, but inaccurate information which affected their credit rating would be a much more serious matter. Similarly, inaccurate information on a police computer which was made available to a potential employer would be equally damaging.

4 *Individuals should have the right to check the details of records held on them.*

   However, herein lies a problem. An individual may not know that a particular computer record exists, which makes it impossible to question the accuracy of the information. Secondly, it is sometimes argued that it is not in the public interest to allow the public access to records.

Security

Privacy and security go hand in hand. If sensitive information is not to be freely available to unauthorised users, measures must be taken to make the information secure.

The most obvious first step is to isolate the information. Perhaps, only authorised users of the computer system will be allowed into the computer building or into the data centre. This can involve having a security guard to check identity cards and log visits or using electronic badge readers.

The computer software itself can be used to thwart those who breach the first stage in security. It is possible to make files available to only those who key in a valid password – a different one for each file. These passwords need to be changed regularly, systematically but unpredictably.

Some authorised users will attempt to extract information from the system for reasons other than those for which it was intended. They may be deterred if an *audit trail* is built into the system. Each request for information is logged by the computer and, since the user will only gain access to the information through a personal user code, which unambiguously identifies him or her, any misuse of the system can be traced back to that person.

A further security measure is to give personnel different levels of security clearance. Again using a password, some will have access to some of the information, others access to a good deal of the information, and a few to all of it.

Some unauthorised disclosures of information may be the result of opportunism – an opportunity presents itself and someone takes advantage of it. A legitimate user may forget to log out. The computer can, however, be programmed to shut down the terminal after a period of inactivity.

During the course of a working day, much information may be output to a printer, although its useful life may be very short. There is little point in elaborate security procedures if the printout is thrown out with the coffee cups and general office waste. The answer is a shredder.

An important element in data security is personnel education. The education program will seek to raise the security consciousness of staff, encouraging them to behave correctly and responsibly. It will also ensure that all staff are adequately trained in security procedures and made aware of the consequences of inefficiency in this respect.

Index

record 6, 17, 19, 22, 27, 34, 73, 103, 108

sector 65
security 79, 110
sequential 61
serial access 61
software 76, 110
source 27, 31–36
statistics 72

terminal 19, 58
time-sharing 79
track 65

transaction file 73
truncation 30, 48

updating 17, 48, 73, 74, 79

validation 14, 46, 70
visual display unit (VDU) 57

wand 16, 18
weighting 13
Winchester disks 19, 66
word processing 81